Restoring Your
Spiritual Heritage

Restoring Your
Spiritual Heritage

Lessons from the Woman at the Well

JULIE R. WILSON

FaithWalk
PUBLISHING

Grand Haven, Michigan

©2004 Julie R. Wilson
Published by FaithWalk Publishing
Grand Haven, Michigan 49417

Printed in the United States of America

09 08 07 06 05 04   7 6 5 4 3 2 1

Library of Congress Cataloging-in-Publication Data

Wilson, Julie R.
  Restoring your spiritual heritage: lessons from the woman at the well / by Julie R. Wilson.—1st ed.
    p. cm.
  ISBN 1-932902-44-9 (pbk. : alk. paper)
  1. Samaritan woman (Biblical figure) 2. Sanctification—Biblical teaching—Textbooks.
3. Christian women—Religious life—Textbooks. 4. Bible. N.T. John—Textbooks. I. Title.
  BS2520.S9W55 2004
  248.8'43—dc22
            2004011588

Dedication

I dedicate this book to all the women who will find
something of themselves within its pages.

May you be encouraged to seek the Lord's restoration
and ministry for your lives.

God bless you.

Acknowledgments

I give all credit for the wisdom and skill of this project to the Holy Spirit of my Lord Jesus Christ, who is the only Teacher. I thank You for the privilege of watching You work.

I also wish to thank my husband, Keith, and my children, Alexia and Samuel, for your patience and support throughout this project. Keith, I love you dearly. Your faith in the Lord and his calling upon my life has sustained me on many a late night when I wanted to call it quits. Thank you for maintaining high standards in your own life and in our home. Truly, you are a man of God and I am blessed to be called your wife.

Thank you to Janice Williams and the ladies of the "Women at the Well" Bible studies, who encouraged me throughout the difficult task of putting this study on paper. Your insights and enthusiasm have both challenged and inspired me to continue the race.

Thank you to my dear friends, mentors, and co-laborers: Kathy, Polliana, Candy, Colleen, Tomi, Nita, and many others for your listening ears and loving hearts when I have needed, and truly needed, guidance. You have been my Aaron and Hur. Thank you.

Thank you to Dirk, Louann, Ginny, Sheila, and the rest of the team at FaithWalk for making this book a stronger final product than it first began. How precious it is to work with such gifted and sensitive vessels. May God give you a good return for your labor.

Table of Contents

Introduction

This study addresses the issue of restoration. The word "restore" means: (1) to bring back into existence or use; (2) to bring back to an original condition; (3) to put (someone) back in a prior position; or (4) to make restitution: to give back (*American Heritage Dictionary*). Isaiah 61:4 states "They [the people of God] will rebuild the ancient ruins and restore the places long devastated; they will renew the ruined cities that have been devastated for generations." This verse (along with the rest of Chapter 61) speaks of the last days' church and suggests a measure of restoration among the people of God which exceeds our greatest imaginations. The Lord is eager to heal His people, both men and women. He is eager to restore our inheritance in Him.

Most of us are not experiencing the fullness of our inheritance in Jesus Christ simply because we have no idea what that really means or how to go about claiming it. Like the woman at the well in John 4, we live like outcasts to the kingdom of God. This study focuses on the story of the woman at the well and the manner in which Jesus systematically restored this Samaritan woman from being an outcast to becoming the evangelist of her entire town. The four stages of this process (which we will study in depth) are as follows:

1. The *invitation* to accept living water,
2. The necessity of dealing with the *past*,
3. The establishment of covenant *relationship*, and
4. The *release* for ministry in Jesus's name.

The study comprises twelve lessons that may be adjusted for personal or group use. All text and study materials have been compiled into this book for your convenience. The only materials required to complete the study are this book, a pen, and a readable Bible version. While blanks have been provided to answer questions at the end of each lesson, you may wish to purchase a notebook to record your answers and reflections to study prompts.

Each lesson will include homework assignments. These assignments are not mandatory but are strongly suggested. You will get out of this study what you put in to it. Homework assignments provide key Scriptures for further study, with questions to guide your reflection. In your book or notebook, you may record any significant questions, thoughts, or reactions you may have to these passages. Occasionally, suggestions for targeted prayer or meditation are offered to help you process and apply the scriptural truths this study investigates.

At any point in your study, if you feel you need additional help, I encourage you to discuss your feelings with a class instructor, pastor, trained counselor, or mature Christian friend. Sometimes the issues of our pasts can cause us to stumble, and we need the support of one another to put these matters into perspective and prayerfully overcome their unhealthy influences. As the Bible states in Ecclesiastes 4:9–10, "Two are better than one, because they have a good return for their work. If one falls down, his friend can help him up." May the Holy Spirit reside with you and help you as you study God's Word in these pages.

Julie R. Wilson

What is
Restoration?

1

This study focuses on *restoration*, a timely and important spiritual concept. Specifically, we will be looking at God's plan for the restoration of women. Women today desperately need restoration. In the presence of a soaring divorce rate and a plague of nonbiblical ideologies, many women feel confused and broken. Many are beginning to lose hope. In disappointment, they ask, "Where did I go wrong? What did I do to deserve this? How did I end up here? Why do I feel so unsatisfied?"

These questions ring much like those that the Samaritan woman of John 4 may have asked. After five husbands and the experience of being ostracized by her entire town, she must have wondered what went wrong. Lonely and despairing, she sets out for the town well one day, and there she experiences a life-changing encounter with Jesus. Their highly symbolic dialogue reveals a four-stage plan of restoration centering around key issues which illuminate the work of God in women's lives.

Isaiah 61:4 states that the people of God will "restore the ancient ruins and rebuild the places long devastated." In context, this Scripture refers to the mission of Jesus Christ and the ministry of his body, the Church. The "places" referred to in this passage can be understood on two levels: One describes actual geographic locations to be restored to the nation of Israel, and the other refers symbolically to places of emotional and spiritual devastation in human hearts that exist as the result of sin. Through the ministry of Jesus Christ, the devastated places of wounded hearts can be healed and restored. He is our Hope and our Healer.

In John 4, Jesus guides the woman at the well to just such restoration through four distinct stages. These stages, as detailed in the story, are the *invitation* to accept living water, the necessity of dealing with the *past*, the establishment of covenant *relationship*, and the *release* for ministry in Jesus's name. We will study each stage sequentially along with relevant accounts of similar restoration recorded in other Scripture passages.

It is my sincere hope and desire that this study will challenge you to go deeper in your relationship with Jesus Christ. Truly, He is the beginning and end of all that we are or hope to be. In him, we can find rest for our souls and lay to rest those things that hinder us from obtaining intimacy with God. This process is not always easy, but the end results far outweigh any temporary discomfort we may feel as we confront the lies and strongholds that have tainted our perceptions and enslaved us to false identities. As we begin to discover who we are in Jesus, to uncover and unearth the long devastated places of our hearts, we will marvel at the plan of God and the deep love that He has for each one whom He has so carefully constructed. Through this process, many of us will come to know ourselves for the first time.

The Bible says that you and I are the Bride of Christ (Is 62:5; Rv 19:7). We are the Lord's inheritance, just as He is ours (Jer 10:16; Eph 1:18). We are what He longs for, dreams about, and rejoices over day and night (Zeph 3:17). These ideas can be overwhelming, yet they are true and their truth has power to change lives.

As we begin to discover our spiritual heritage, we will no longer be so easily swayed to believe the enemy's lies regarding all that we are not or have failed to become. We will no longer bow so easily to his relentless assault on our minds, hearts, and families. As we develop an understanding of who we are and all that we possess in Jesus, we will learn to fight back. We will learn to stand with confidence upon the truth of God's Word and overcome the adversary of our souls (Rv 12:10). Most importantly, we will be released to approach the throne of grace more intimately and passionately, because we will no longer feel condemned by false accusations and self-doubt, wondering if God really does love us as his Word proclaims. We will know that we know that we know: Jesus is "God with us" and we are precious to him.

What does it mean to be restored? In a biblical sense, restoration refers to the process of being *sanctified* or made complete in Christ (Jn 17:19–24). Throughout the Bible, God commands us to be holy even as He is holy (Lev 11:44; 1 Pt 1:14–16). God desires to restore us to complete perfection, without weakness or fault. Ephesians 5:25–27 states that Christ is returning for a Bride without spot or wrinkle. Because He is able, the Lord strives earnestly to make us whole and set us apart for him; to "sanctify" us.

In the past, many men and women received teaching on sanctification that was infiltrated with some degree of *legalism*. In other words, they were instructed (or they interpreted) that they were responsible for achieving God's perfection on their own. Somewhere deep inside their hearts, a nagging little voice sprang up saying, "Work harder, work harder, work harder," or "You can only approach God when you have conquered this or that area of your life."

Nothing lies further from the truth of God's Word. The Bible says, "All have sinned and fall short of the glory of God" (Rom 3:23). Your weakness, even your most horrendous thought or failure, is no surprise to God. Nothing you have ever done has shocked him. The Bible says, "No temptation has seized you except what is *common* to man" (1 Cor 10:13). Remember, God is the Ancient of Days—He has seen it all!

I say this to encourage you: Don't be afraid of the Lord. As we confront the issues of our past and present lives, remember that God loves you more than you can imagine (Eph 3:20). Zephaniah 3:17 states that He dances over you with great joy. No matter where you are right now or where you have been before, the Lord is eager to receive you and to restore to you all that has been lost through time, painful relationships, and sin. He knows you more intimately than you know yourself (Ps 139:13–16), and He wants to help you become far more than you ever dreamed you were meant to be.

God is on your side—always. Deuteronomy 31:6 promises that He will never leave you or forsake you. No matter what—He will not willingly give you up (though He will allow you to walk away). As long as you draw near to him, with whatever faltering or misguided steps you can muster, He will draw near to you (Jas 4:8). Furthermore, by his continual outpouring of spirit and truth, He will set you free. He will heal your land (2 Chr 7:14).

I believe that the Lord is eager to restore the inheritance of his people. Most of us are not experiencing the fullness of our inheritance simply because we have no idea what that really means or how to go about claiming it. Like the woman at the well in John 4, we live like outcasts from the kingdom of God. Periodically, we find ourselves facing dry situations with a well of emptied resources.

Even though we may have professed a belief in Christ (as she does in John 4:25), we are plagued by a deep inner thirsting, which no amount of confession, sacrifice, or change can fully quench. In honest moments of personal reflection, we may admit feeling, "Surely, there must be more than this." More power to fight Satan's relentless attacks, more opportunity for intimate fellowship with God and others, more confidence than I seem able to sustain, more certainty of why I am here and what I am gifted to do, more success at marriage or motherhood than I experience on a daily basis … "More, Lord, give me more."

Have you ever felt this way? I know I have and still do sometimes. After all, restoration is a process that may take a lifetime to complete. However, that should not discourage us from beginning the journey. The path of restoration leads straight to the heart of God. As we grow in our knowledge of him, of his ways, and of all He made us to be, we regain our spiritual sight and begin to experience life on entirely new levels. With each new revelation, a veil is lifted, enabling us to enter into deeper relationship both with God and others.

It is an exciting journey, one worth taking. So let's begin.

Scripture Study

Read John 4:1–26 (the woman at the well).

1. Have you ever heard a sermon or other teaching on this passage?

2. What are your initial impressions of this woman? Can you relate to her? In what way?

Read Isaiah 61 and Luke 4:16–21. The passage from Isaiah is quoted in part by Jesus in the synagogue. Now that He is ascended and we, through the Spirit, are his body, the Isaiah promises apply to us. They describe the ministry and inheritance of the Church in the last days.

1. According to Isaiah 61:1–3, why has the "Spirit of the Sovereign Lord" been given to us?

2. List the "ministries" of the Church recorded in this passage.

3. How many of these ministries are currently taking place in your life?

4. Which ones do you feel most drawn to?

From Isaiah 61:3–11, list the promises God has decreed for his people. These promises summarize the inheritance of the saints and extend the description of the Holy Spirit's "anointing" introduced in verse 1. Which of these promises appeal to you most right now?

Read Proverbs 3:5–6.

1. In verses 5 and 6, the writer gives three instructions that lead to "straight paths." What are they? In your own words, rewrite this proverb.

2. Now read verse 26 of Chapter 3. Who or what is to be our confidence?

It is important to know (in our heads) the elements of our spiritual heritage in Jesus Christ. However, it is equally important that we develop confidence (in our hearts) to exercise authority as partakers of that heritage. Throughout this study, we will be seeking not only to understand the elements of our spiritual heritage, but also to remove the stumbling blocks which inhibit our confidence in applying these elements to our lives and the lives of our families.

Ask the Holy Spirit to identify one stumbling block that is inhibiting you from exercising your spiritual heritage. Record his answer.

Reflection

Which of the previous Scripture passages (John 4, Isaiah 61, or Proverbs 3:5–6,26) speaks to you most right now?

If the Lord spoke to you directly, what do you think He would say to you about your life at this season? What are your needs? What are your challenges?

What "ruined cities" or "long devastated places" can you identify in women's lives today? In your own life?

Write at least one specific way you would like to grow through this study?

Facing the Noonday Heat

The Story 2 of Hagar

In the first lesson, I introduced the story of the woman at the well as a symbolic account of God's plan to restore Christian women. Some time ago, as I was praying for direction concerning an upcoming Bible study I was scheduled to teach, I asked the Lord, "Father, what is your heart for women? What would you like to tell them?" The Holy Spirit responded, *"Restore their spiritual heritage."* I was surprised at the frankness of his answer. "Great, Lord," I said, "But what does that mean? What is a *spiritual heritage*?"

Having not grown up in a Christian home, my idea of spiritual heritage was fuzzy at best. So I called a good friend whom I knew had grown up in a strong Christian home. "Michele," I asked, "what does it mean to have a spiritual heritage, and how do you develop that in your children?" My wonderful Nebraska friend thought for a moment, then launched into a series of stories about her mom, a woman of strong convictions with a deep love for God. She told me how her mother used to put all five kids in bed and go pass out Christian tracts at the local dance club. Michele also shared how hard her mother had worked to love each child individually and how each of her brothers and sisters had responded differently to their mother's home-based ministry. Some of them, like Michele, embraced salvation at an early age and remained true to the Lord ever since. Others, like her two younger brothers, remained spiritually aloof despite their Christian upbringing.

Michele shared many different stories, but we both struggled to glean from them exactly how to define a spiritual heritage or identify how such an identity could be handed down from one generation to the next. All in all, the process seemed sort of nebulous.

I left that conversation with more questions than answers. So I kept praying, "Lord, please show me what it means to possess and restore a spiritual heritage." I bought a notebook and I began making notes of every time in Scripture the words *heritage* or *inheritance* appeared. The list seemed endless. Then, a still, small voice began directing me to the woman at the well. Over and over, I read her story. Each time I saw things I hadn't seen before—similarities to modern life, powerful symbolic word plays, and a striking number of "theological" issues addressed within the short span of one chapter in the Gospel of John.

What's more, each new reading helped me to see this woman differently. In the past, I had heard sermons and references based on this passage many times. Most of them presented the woman at the well as a prostitute or woman of ill repute who was avoiding Jesus's interrogation by fending off his questions with defiance and doubt. I had rarely heard anything more said of her, yet as I read and re-read this passage I discovered there was much more to this nameless woman. And much more to be learned from her story ...

For one thing, she is given nearly an entire chapter in the Bible. Clearly, John the Beloved understood that hers was no ordinary encounter. First of all, she was a Samaritan; at that time, Jews simply did not associate with impure Samaritans. Secondly, she was a woman, a second-class citizen of mixed blood. Furthermore, she was poor (or she would have had servants fetching her water), unmarried (Jn 4:18), and socially ostracized. She had nothing to offer Jesus—absolutely nothing.

Two things we must remember about the Gospel of John. First, it is dramatically abbreviated, one of the shortest gospel accounts (superseded only by Mark). Secondly, the Book of John is highly symbolic. John, perhaps better than any other Gospel writer, understood the interplay of natural and supernatural woven together throughout Jesus's life on earth. In his account of Christ's life, John sought to provide insight into these dual realities rather than provide thorough journalistic accounts. He was more concerned about thematic and conceptual truths than factual comprehensiveness. We see these interests expressed in his presentation of the Samaritan woman.

She was no ordinary woman, and yet she typifies all women. On the surface, her story is not ordinary, yet the issues it reveals touch the heart of every human being. When we look closer, we see in her something of ourselves—not in prostitution but in her spiritual prostration. She comes to Jesus when she is at the end of her rope. She has tried everything else, and everything else has failed her.

As we explore this and other related stories of restoration in the Word, it is important to look beyond the circumstances of these individuals' lives. Do not be distracted by time period, social class, moral stature, gender, or other external features. Rather, I exhort you: Look deeper. You may be surprised to find that these individuals had the same questions and struggles in their relationships with God that we all have.

In the opening scene of the woman at the well, John writes:

> *The Pharisees heard that Jesus was gaining and baptizing more disciples than John, although in fact it was not Jesus who baptized, but his disciples. When the Lord learned of this, he left Judea and went back once more to Galilee. Now he had to go through Samaria. So he came to a town in Samaria called Sychar, near the plot of ground Jacob had given to his son Joseph. Jacob's well was there, and Jesus, tired as he was from the journey, sat down by the well. It was about the sixth hour. (v. 1–6)*

Frustrated with the relentless, petty criticism of the Pharisees, Jesus decides to go back to Galilee. The Scripture states that He "had to go through Samaria," which isn't exactly true. There was an alternate route which religious Jews would have taken in order to avoid becoming "unclean" by passing through Samaritan territory. However, Jesus had his own reasons for passing through Samaria, which will be seen shortly. Tired from the journey, Jesus sits down by a well outside of Sychar while his disciples go into town to buy food. It is about noon (v. 6).

After a while, we don't know how long, a woman comes to draw water. She is an outcast woman from a mixed-blood race. There is a half-empty well. And rising heat. On many levels, both individual and corporate, this Samaritan woman delivers a poignant illustration of the plight of the modern day Church.

Yet before we enter her dialogue with Jesus, let us flash back to another woman, Hagar, whose life was also changed by a "well" experience. Genesis 16 records her story.

Genesis 16 opens with Sarah accusing God of withholding his promise. She tells Abraham, in so many words, "God has kept me from having children, so I have an idea." She's off to a bad start, and it gets worse. Sarah suggests that Abraham take Hagar, Sarah's Egyptian maidservant, as a wife and lie with her to produce children. This was actually a common practice among the Middle Eastern people of that time and of the locale where Abraham and Sarah had moved at God's command. For all natural purposes, Sarah's plan seemed logical.

Hagar was an Egyptian slave, a woman of color, who had been given to Abraham (and ultimately to Sarah) by Pharaoh as part of the ruler's payoff for having taken Sarah as a wife. Notice the similarity: Sarah was given Hagar for having been taken wrongly and now she is wrongly giving Hagar to be taken. Hagar had no say in this ill-fated arrangement. Once she had conceived, Hagar began to despise Sarah; Sarah, in turn, mistreated Hagar. In desperation, Hagar fled to a well in the desert where an angel of the Lord appeared to her. The angel asked Hagar two important questions: "Hagar, servant of Sarai, where have you come from and where are you going?" (Gn 16:8)

Many women today are like Hagar. They have been deeply wounded, mistreated by life, and they have run. In an emotional sense, these women have fled to the desert of despair, and the Lord is seeking them out with the same questions He posed to Hagar: "Where have you come from, and where are you going? Are you going to continue the rest of your life like this, or are you ready to change? Are you thirsty for more than what you have yet experienced?"

Like Hagar, many of us cannot fully answer these questions. In Genesis 16:8, Hagar responds only to the first question, saying, "I'm running away from my mistress, Sarai." Either because she had not decided her final destination or because she knew her flight home to Egypt (in which direction she was headed) was wrong, Hagar ignores the angel's second query. Like many of us today, Hagar responded to harsh circumstances with a knee-jerk reaction; and now she is challenged to consider the ramifications of her decision.

How often we forget our role in the great script of God and succumb to the temptation of viewing our current situations as loose ends that we need to tie up. When hardships press in, how often we run. Like Hagar, we flee the pain and forget the promise. To obtain stability in our relationship with God and in other areas of our lives, we must learn to keep hold of the greater picture. This is the lesson of Hagar.

We can learn much from our sister Hagar about restoration. After all, we all fall off the horse from time to time. No matter how "spiritual" we become, our humanness leaves us vulnerable to all sorts of physical, emotional, and relational setbacks. It is not uncommon for even the greatest men and women of God to find themselves occasionally in the desert (*see* 1 Kgs 19). In Genesis 16:9, the angel of the Lord gives Hagar clear directions regarding how to get out of the desert and back onto the pathway of life. Let's take a moment to study these directions.

First, the angel tells Hagar, "Go back." For the healing process to begin, we must quit running and face our accusers and our past. God does not condemn us for running away; He is merciful and understands our weakness. While He may sympathize with our pain, however, He cannot condone our continued flight. Thus, as odd as it may seem at the time, it is God who commands our return. In Hagar's case, He commands her to return to slavery.

Secondly, the angel declares, "Submit to your mistress." In other words, we must submit, with discernment from the Holy Spirit, to the Lord's anointed instruments and plans for our change. Both for our sakes and those who follow (especially our children), we cannot run from the painful circumstances of our lives. We must stick it out until we obtain a "right release" from these difficulties. Otherwise, God's healing for us will be hindered, and we will not be free to enter new phases of life. If Hagar had continued to run, she would have lived out her life as an escaped slave, with the fear of discovery forever haunting her. Unresolved issues in our lives function much the same way. They serve as a trap door to our emotions that we try to keep locked but which at any time may suddenly give way. God has a plan to heal and restore each and every area of our lives, but we must submit to *his* way for that healing to be accomplished.

Finally, the angel gives Hagar a promise of great blessing for her obedience. This promise would be realized later in Ishmael's prosperity and Hagar's freedom. If we submit to God's plan for our lives, no matter how strange at times it may seem, we are assured of great blessing (Eph 3:20). To get out of the desert, we must trust the faithfulness of our God that He really will work all things for our good (Rom 8:28).

Hagar does what the angel instructed and is not mentioned again until Genesis 21. By this point, Sarah has borne Isaac, the child of promise, and wishes to rid herself once and for all of Hagar and Ishmael. The Lord instructs Abraham to comply with Sarah's demand; Hagar and Ishmael are sent back into the desert. When their water runs out, Hagar sets her son under a bush and moves away to avoid watching him die. They both begin to cry out to the Lord. The Lord, whom she had earlier named "the God Who Sees Me" hears their cries and speaks to Hagar with assuring words of his faithfulness to fulfill all that He promised. Then He opens her eyes to a well of water and saves them. Once again, the Lord meets Hagar at a well in the desert and reveals his love.

There are significant similarities between the story of Hagar and the story of the Samaritan woman in John 4. Both occur near a well, in a desert, in the heat of day. Both involve women who are not Jews, who lived as outcasts. Both were broken women, torn asunder by abusive or abandoned relations with men. Both were functionally at the end of themselves and in desperate need of a Savior.

Modern day women have much in common with these sisters who lived centuries ago. Though we no longer seek wells for water, many of us have sought fulfillment from a variety of different resources. Some of these include marriages, careers, social status, material possessions, education, children, even church or volunteer work. According to Ruth Senter, author of *Have We Really Come A Long Way: Regaining What Feminism Has Stolen From Christian Women*, the primary well for many women is simply busy-ness. We hide behind hectic lives to avoid the responsibility of reflection, through which we attach meaning to our lives and face the possibility that we may have veered off course somewhere. In so doing, we expose ourselves to great danger. For, as Senter notes, "A life without contemplation quickly loses depth. It becomes like a field that is all topsoil—one strong wind and it is all blown away" (Bethany House, 1997, p.115).

While these "wells" in themselves are not wrong, they cannot ultimately quench the thirsting of our spirits. Thus, we find ourselves, like the woman at the well, frustrated by the continual need that never seems to be satisfied, only driven deeper as the disappointments of life stack up.

It is time we face our deserts. If we, like Hagar, will surrender these dry places in our lives, these "walls" (for that is what *Shur*, the original name of the well where Hagar first met the Lord, means), the Lord will bring them down. Despite the hardships Hagar encountered, both before and after her meeting with the angel, she ended her life as a free woman. Moreover, many generations continued to be blessed for her faithfulness. Just as the Lord promised, Ishmael and his descendants arose as a mighty nation (Gn 21:18).

The first time Hagar entered the desert, it was her choice to do so. The second time was not. Whether by choice or circumstances, God faithfully met her in miraculous ways. Likewise, whether our deserts come from our own mistakes or those of others, God can restore us in and through them. In his love, He may allow us to wander for a season, to experience the noonday heat until all our water (representing our own resources) runs out, but He will never let us die there. He is our Well, *Beer-lahai-roi*, which means the "Well of the Living One, My Seer" (Gn 16:13–14).

Scripture Study

Read Genesis 16. Try to put yourself in Hagar's shoes.

1. How would you have felt to be forced into this arrangement between Sarah and Abraham?

2. Have you ever been strongly encouraged to go along with something you knew wouldn't work?

3. How did you feel about the people who put you up to it when it finally failed?

4. How does Hagar perceive God in the desert? Does she feel condemned? How do we know?

5. What two things does the angel tell Hagar to do? What does this suggest about how restoration begins?

6. What eventually happens to Hagar and Ishmael? Who does Ishmael represent?

Read 1 Kings 19.

1. Why does Elijah flee to the desert?

2. What incident immediately precedes Elijah's flight? (*see* 1 Kgs 18)

3. How does the Lord receive Elijah in the desert? Identify the similarities between Elijah's desert experience and Hagar's.

4. What point is the Lord trying to make in the wind, earthquake, fire, and whisper that Elijah needed to understand? What does the Lord direct Elijah to do that parallels his instructions to Hagar?

Read John 4:4–15.
1. In this initial scene, what is the main topic of discussion?

2. Why does Jesus ask her for a drink? What is He *really* asking?

3. How does this inquiry compare to what the angels asked both Hagar and Elijah? Why does God ask us questions?

Reflection

In your book or notebook, describe any "noonday experiences" you have had in your life. How did you respond: Did you run to the desert, to the well, or both? What did you learn about yourself through those experiences? What did you learn about God through those experiences?

Based on these and other experiences you have had with the Lord, what sort of personal name could you give him (as Hagar does with "God Who Sees Me")? Naming the Lord is an act of worship. Take time to present this name to the Lord in prayer and praise him for his faithfulness.

Consider the following question: How does one restore a building that is no longer structurally sound? How does this compare to God's plan for restoring us? Based on what you have learned in this chapter, what is the first step to restoration? What does it *really* mean to "go back"? How does that apply to your life?

A Strange
Invitation

Natural vs.
Supernatural

In this lesson, we will investigate the dual nature of reality as it is portrayed throughout Scripture and experienced throughout life. One of Jesus's main objectives in many of his recorded conversations with individuals (including the woman at the well) simply involved helping people understand this crucial aspect of mortal existence. Simply stated, we live simultaneously in two worlds: a natural world and a supernatural, or spiritual, world. Whatever decisions or actions we perform in one realm significantly affect life in the parallel sphere. These two realities are distinct yet inseparable.

The natural world includes all physical matter such as dirt, grass, trees, people, animals, and all man-made technologies. This is the world that we relate to through our physical bodies, senses, emotions, and intellect. It represents tangible, concrete reality, which for most of us comprises life as we have known it.

The supernatural or spiritual realm, on the other hand, remains far less experienced by most Christians. This realm is predominantly invisible to human eyes yet functions all around us. Chuck Smith, in *Living Water*, describes the spirit realm this way: "[The Bible] tells us there are two worlds coexisting, each passing through the other. For the most part, we are not conscious of that other world—but it is very conscious of us. The Bible calls it the world of spirits. This spiritual world is very real, and has a tremendous influence on all of our lives, either for good or for evil" (Harvest House, 1996, p.164).

Jesus Christ is Lord of both natural and supernatural reality. Absolutely nothing in either realm lies outside his jurisdiction. Philippians 2:9–11 states that Jesus has been given "the Name that is above every name, that at the name of Jesus every knee should bow, *in heaven and on earth and under the earth*, and every tongue confess that Jesus Christ is Lord, to the glory of God the Father" (emphasis added).

Now before I lose anyone, let me explain the purpose of establishing these truths. I do not intend to start calling down demons or launch you unprepared into full-fledged spiritual warfare. In fact, my concern at this point has little to do with either angels or demons. I simply wish, as Jesus did in John 4, to open your eyes and expose your mind to dual-reality thinking.

If there is one concept I hope you take with you from this study, it involves understanding how to discern between natural and supernatural reality. Knowing how to separate and perceptually define these coexisting worlds will enable you to identify the crucial issues at stake in any situation or scriptural passage. In the Bible, this gift is called "discernment" and is usually applied to distinguishing between clean (angelic) and unclean (demonic) spiritual influences affecting an individual's life. When used to identify evil in a general sense (such as in Proverbs), this gift is associated with wisdom and serves to encourage righteous behavior. Francis Frangipane, in *The Three Battlegrounds*, defines discernment as "our capacity to perceive correctly" (p. 55). He goes on to say "spiritual discernment is the grace to see into the unseen. It is a gift *of the Spirit* to see what is *in the spirit*. Its purpose is to see into the nature of that which is veiled" (Arrow Publications, 1989, p. 56).

For our immediate purposes, we will limit discernment to understanding the symbolic relationship between things in the "natural" and issues in the "supernatural" which those things represent. For example, water in the natural often represents the Holy Spirit and the degree to which He is being allowed to direct individual or corporate circumstances. Storms in the natural signify unrest in the heart (where the spirit of man resides) and indicates the struggle of flesh and spirit which often dominates man's experience. Famine represents spiritual poverty. Fire may symbolize either judgment or cleansing of spiritual corruption. Fruit represents blessing. The list could go on and on.

I stated earlier that there are two things to remember about the Book of John: It is abbreviated, and it is symbolic. The writer of this Gospel, perhaps more than any other Gospel writer, understood the centrality of dual-reality thinking to Jesus's life and ministry. John possessed great discernment regarding the underlying spiritual issues that Jesus sought to expose and heal. John frequently looked "beyond the natural" in his writings to expound the spiritual truths that Jesus, in all that He said, did, and even was, represented.

For those who have experienced some level of symbolism in God's Word, what I am saying is not entirely new. But let's take that experience one step further. Rather than studying word-level symbolism, let's seek to discern the alternate reality that those symbols, once combined, represent. For example, let's look at John 4:4–14. This is the opening scene of the woman at the well. Jesus initiates conversation with a strange woman by asking her for a drink. She replies, "You are a Jew and I am a Samaritan woman. How can you ask me for a drink?" So far, their conversation dwells primarily in the natural.

Suddenly, however, Jesus shifts gears: "If you knew the gift of God and who it is that asks you for a drink, you would have asked him and he would have given you living water." The woman doesn't get it. She remains in the natural, replying, "You have nothing to draw with and the well is deep. Where can you get this living water?" Jesus extends an enticing invitation: He offers her "water" that will quench all thirsting and even become a perpetual spring within (v. 13–14).

Although it takes the woman several more verses before she figures out that Jesus is talking about something quite beyond natural reality, she begins to detect something in his offer that sparks her interest. Her spirit is awakening from the slumber of sin's death. Something strange yet familiar beckons her to proceed.

Deep within each of us lies a thirsting for the supernatural. From the beginning, we were created to operate in both realms. This was the unique and awesome call of mankind, the only creature who was "made in the likeness of God" (Gn 1:26–27). As a result of the Fall, however, we lost our transcending capacity. Even as our eyes opened to the knowledge of good and evil, they became closed to the greater realities of eternal life, with all its spiritual implications (Gn 3:7–24).

So it has continued through today for many people. We perceive natural reality plainly, but spiritually we are blind. Thus, we establish our lives according to natural "laws," forsaking the greater laws of the Spirit. God is Spirit (Jn 4:24) which means that spiritual reality predominates its natural counterpart (1 Cor 15:50). All natural reality shall someday cease, but spiritual reality is everlasting (Ps 148:6; Mt 24:35) Thus, to experience breakthrough in our lives, to obtain the intimacy we desire with God and others, and to quench the inner thirsting that nothing in the natural seems to satisfy, we must first regain our sensitivity to spiritual matters.

Luke 19:10 states that Jesus came "to seek and to save that which was lost." When we take a closer look at Jesus's ministry, specifically at the few recorded conversations He had with individuals, we see the priority He placed upon awakening spiritual sensitivity. We can trace this emphasis throughout the story of the woman at the well, yet she is neither the first nor the last person whom Jesus worked diligently to revive. As we become accustomed to dual-reality thinking, we recognize that while Jesus faithfully addressed the "natural" needs of those who came to him (i.e., He provided healing, food, and instruction), his ultimate ministry addressed deeper spiritual needs and issues. Jesus did not deny the natural; rather, He worked through it to restore awareness of the spiritual.

Unfortunately, while Jesus understood this dual purpose, many who came to him did not. For example, John 3 recalls the story of Nicodemus, a man who possessed great natural knowledge yet struggled to comprehend even the simplest spiritual truths. John 3:1 tells us that Nicodemus was a member of the Jewish ruling council, known as the Sanhedrin. Thus, we know that Nicodemus was wealthy, well educated, and respected as a prominent public figure. He comes to Jesus at night to inquire about the miraculous signs that told him Jesus is a "teacher who has come from God" (v. 2).

Jesus doesn't beat around the bush. In verse 3, He goes straight for Nicodemus's heart when he says, "I tell you the truth, no one can see the kingdom of God unless he is born again." The word for "see" that Jesus used means "to know," and the word used for "born again" bears a distinct suggestion of "regeneration." Thus, Jesus effectively says, "Forget it, Nicodemus. No one can understand the kingdom of God (which is spiritual) unless he has been spiritually regenerated."

Unfortunately, Jesus's analogy doesn't translate, and Nicodemus misses the point. Instead, he begins to argue with God Incarnate regarding what is and is not impossible, naturally speaking. Jesus plays along to some degree until verse 6 when He plainly states, "Flesh gives birth to flesh, but the Spirit gives birth to spirit. You should not be surprised at my saying, 'You must be born again.' The wind blows wherever it pleases. You hear its sound, but you cannot tell where it comes from or where it is going. So it is with everyone born of the Spirit" (v. 6–8).

Nicodemus is dumbfounded. "How can this be?" he asks.

Jesus replies somewhat critically, "You are Israel's teacher ... and do you not understand these things? ... I have spoken to you of earthly things [that is, things pertaining to natural life on earth] and you do not believe; how then will you believe if I speak of heavenly [spiritual] things?" (v. 9–12). Jesus continues by outlining the whole plan of salvation. He ends by saying, "This is the verdict: Light has come into the world, but men loved darkness instead of light because their deeds were evil. Everyone who does evil hates the light, and will not come into the light for fear that his deeds will be exposed. But whoever lives by the truth comes into the light, so that it may be seen plainly that what he has done has been done through God" (v. 19-21).

These words must have stung Nicodemus even as they spilled from the Savior's mouth. After all, Nicodemus had come to Jesus at night for fear of being exposed. He was an upstanding member of the religious sect that Jesus publicly criticized on more than one occasion. Yet something within him recognized Jesus—that strange yet familiar feeling of an awakened spirit. Thus, he comes to Jesus, but only half-committed. He wants answers in the natural for things that may only be understood by the Spirit. Jesus presents him with a great challenge: "Step into the light" and live by truth. Take a stand for the spiritual even though it makes no natural sense (1 Cor 1:18–21). For this is faith, by which the "just shall live" (Gal 3:11).

We are never told what happens to Nicodemus. He reappears twice in Jesus's life, once in John 7:50, attempting to protect Jesus by arguing legalities with the Pharisees, and again in John 19:39, helping Joseph of Arimathaea to provide a hasty burial for Jesus's crucified flesh. For all practical purposes, it would seem that Nicodemus became a Christian, albeit an undercover one.

The story of Nicodemus shares a number of interesting similarities with the Samaritan woman's story in Chapter 4. In the natural, these two individuals represent opposites. He is wealthy; she is poor. He is educated; she is not. He is a man of high social standing; she is an outcast. He is a pure blood Jew and Pharisee; she is a mixed blood Samaritan and divorcee. On the surface, they share nothing in common.

Spiritually, however, they are equals. They come to the Lord needing answers. Their lives have been a futile attempt to quiet a raging inner need. Though they approached that need from opposite ends of the spectrum (Nicodemus went the religious performance/perfectionist route; the woman at the well tried the hedonistic/relationship route), the effect remains the same. Their confessions echo the words of Solomon: "Meaningless, meaningless … Everything is meaningless" (Eccl 1:2).

Likewise, Jesus's response to them is equal. Much to Nicodemus's dismay, Jesus does not commend the leader's power, position, education, or religious finesse. Nor does Jesus condemn the woman at the well for her lack of social propriety. Rather, in both cases, the Lord plainly acknowledges their need for total dependence upon God. He makes it clear that "No one comes to the Father except by me" (Jn 14:6).

As biblical scholars have pointed out, when the Lord speaks to Nicodemus of being "born again," He does not mean natural birth, but spiritual. Similarly, when Jesus describes "living water" to the woman at the well, He applies it to an inner thirsting that goes far beyond natural experience. In both stories, the Lord challenges these individuals to address the "real" issues affecting their lives, before He supplies the solution. This suggests that restoration of spiritual sight plays a crucial, even primary, role in the healing of our relationships with God and others. To be set free from whatever inhibits us, we must be awakened spiritually to discern the real issues—separating the natural from the supernatural and giving priority to spiritual causes rather than their natural effects.

As we continue to study the story of the Samaritan woman in John 4, let us identify the "real" issues that Jesus and the woman address. These issues highlight the path of restoration and represent the things we must confront if we are serious about going forward with God. The natural elements of their discussion reveal deep spiritual truth, if we will only view them through spiritual eyes. I encourage you to ask the Lord to apply his salve and open your eyes. Pray that He will give you understanding of spiritual truth and awaken your sensitivity to his Spirit. You will never read Scripture the same way again.

Scripture Study

Read John 3:1–21.

1. Describe your impressions of Nicodemus.

2. Have you ever known anyone like him?

3. What prompts him to come to Jesus? What is he looking for?

4. How does Jesus respond to Nicodemus?

5. Does Jesus give Nicodemus what he wants? Why or why not?

6. What is the "verdict"? (*see* verses 19–21)

Read John 3:20–26. Look at the similarities (both natural and supernatural) between the first and second half of Chapter 3.

1. How does John's understanding of Jesus differ from Nicodemus's?

2. What is it about John that accounts for that difference?

3. Who is John more aligned with spiritually—Jesus or Nicodemus? What does this suggest about spiritual maturity and discernment?

Now read John 4:4–15. Compare Nicodemus to the Samaritan woman.
1. How do they differ in the natural? How are they similar spiritually?

2. How do their responses to Jesus's discussion of "heavenly things" (Jn 3:12) differ? What accounts for this difference?

Turn to Genesis 3:1–19. Notice the many references to "eyes," "see," and "sight" in this account of the fall of man. The fall of man had multiple repercussions, and scholars have suggested many ways to interpret God's judgment in verses 14–19. Let's look at one interpretation.
1. When the serpent said to Eve, "when you eat of [the forbidden fruit], your eyes will be opened and you will be like God" (v. 5), was he lying?

2. What symbolic choice did Eve make in verse 6? What was the result of her choice?

3. How do we continue to face that choice today?

4. How could God's judgment (verses 4–19) be seen as an act of mercy or restitution?

Read 1 Corinthians 15:39–58.
1. In your own words, translate this passage in terms of "natural" and "supernatural" (or spiritual reality).

2. How is the natural "sown" to produce spiritual life?

3. If we know that only the spiritual will last, where should we place our priorities in terms of time, energy, goals, and relationships?

Finally, look at Mark 8:15–29. Again, notice the many references to "eyes," "seeing," "understanding," and "blindness."

1. How does the interjected story of the blind man's healing relate to the accounts of the disciples?

2. What four things does Jesus do to heal the blind man?

3. What are the spiritual parallels to these four steps? What does each step represent?

4. What does it mean to "see people like trees walking around"?

Reflection

What does Colossians 3:1–17 suggest about prioritizing the "spiritual" over the natural? How can this be worked out practically in your own life? In what areas do you need more spiritual discernment and strength?

Have you ever experienced "seeing people as trees"? Do you think this assessment applies to you right now? In what ways do you need God's healing in order to "see" the people in your life more clearly?

Who do you relate to most easily—Nicodemus, John the Baptist, or the woman at the well? What do you think that says about your personality and/or walk with God? Each of these individuals had a major "faith challenge" to overcome in their relationship with Jesus. What do you consider to be the greatest faith challenge in your relationship to Jesus?

Surrendering the
Well of Self

4

In the opening scene of the woman at the well story (Jn 4: 4–15), both the narrator (John) and the woman address the significance of Jacob's well as the setting for this encounter. In this lesson we investigate the history of Jacob's well and the symbolic role that "well experiences" play in restoration.

To begin, there are a couple of interesting facts about Jacob's well worth noting. Jacob's well still exists today, and its authenticity has never been contested with regard to its origin as part of the inheritance that Jacob gave to his son, Joseph. In Scripture, this well is identified, along with the field surrounding it, as the first place Abraham stopped when traveling from Haran to Canaan. God appeared to Abraham there and promised to give the land to his descendants. In response, Abraham built an altar to the Lord and worshipped him.

The Hebrew name for Jacob's well is *El Elohey Yishrael* which means "the Strong God." Whether that name was given by Jacob, I do not know, but it certainly reflects Jacob's relationship with God which was often marked by struggle (*see* Gn 32:28). This well is supplied by runoff from rainfall and snow, and it is located deep within a wall of limestone rock. The well's entrance is so narrow that a man's body can only fit through it when his arms are raised above his head (a significant posture of surrender in worship). Also, the well typically runs dry, and always has, from May until sometime late in the year when the winter rains refill it. Thus, this well represents a rather unstable and often contaminated water supply.

Both John the Beloved and the Samaritan woman emphasize the importance of Jacob's well. Specifically, the woman asks Jesus in verse 12, "Are you greater than our father Jacob, who gave us the well and who drank from it himself, as did also his sons and his flocks and herds?" This is the third and most significant of three questions she poses. To understand this final question, we must comprehend several things.

First, it is important to note that the woman identifies herself with Jacob, calling him "*Our* father Jacob." Samaritans had much to contest with Jews regarding their common kinship and religious practices. The Samaritans were a mixed-blood people who had been brought in under Sargon, the Assyrian King who conquered northern Israel (the territory of Ephraim and Manasseh, Joseph's sons) in 722 B.C. The Samaritan people had as little to do with their being transplanted into Israelite territory as did the Jews who were deported to various parts of Syria and Babylon. When chaos continued to reign in the land, Israelite priests were sent to teach the Samaritans how to worship God, and thus the Samaritans adopted Jewish religious practices (*see* 2 Kgs 17:27).

When the Jews returned from captivity under Ezra and Nehemiah, the Samaritans offered to help rebuild the Jewish temple (Ezra 4:1–10). The Jews staunchly refused. In protest, the Samaritans established their own temple and continued a muddled form of sacrificial worship. Throughout their history, the Samaritans aligned themselves alternately with either the Jews or the Assyrians, depending upon who could offer them the best deal at the moment. For the most part, however, the Samaritans considered themselves to be descendants of Abraham, though the Jews fiercely rejected this claim. Much of the animosity between these two groups stemmed from the Jews' dismissal of Samaritan worship. The woman at the well addresses this issue with Jesus in John 4:20.

When the Samaritan woman challenges Jesus, saying, "Are you greater than Jacob?" she identifies herself as a person who had at least some knowledge of Jewish history. Furthermore, she takes a defensive theological stance. In effect, she says, "So what have you got that I don't already have? Are you saying 'our way' is insufficient?" To better understand this posture, we need to review the surrounding symbolism.

Throughout the story of the Samaritan woman, there exists a powerful symbolic dichotomy between "religion" and "relationship" with Jesus Christ. This dichotomy begins in the opening scene as a wordplay involving a well and a spring (*see* Jn 4:12-14). The differences between these two underground bodies of water provide a powerful word picture. Both wells and springs result from runoff of rain and snow. However, a well is man made, a hole cut into rock (usually limestone) deeper and deeper until it uncovers a groundwater pool. This pool is both stagnant and limited. Furthermore, it is frequently contaminated by mud and other debris that falls into the well or seeps through the soft layers of limestone surrounding it.

A spring, on the other hand, is considered "living" because the water flows continuously, moving in from deeper, distant resources. A spring forms when groundwater is pressed through deep, narrow passages in underground rock layers until gravity forces it upward and causes it to bubble up through the earth's surface. Typically, springs are located at cracks or fissures along the slopes or valleys of mountain passages.

Spiritually, a well represents religion, man's attempt to find and contain God. On the other hand, a spring represents God's design through the Holy Spirit to "find" and flow through man. Thus, when the woman asks, "Are you greater than Jacob, who gave us this well and drank from it himself?" she is really seeking the same answers that Nicodemus sought in John 3. Both of them struggled to fit Jesus into their preconceived religious paradigms. Clearly, He was a "teacher come from God" (Jn 3:2) but just what kind of God did He represent? He did not speak as their past teachers but as One who had authority (Mt 7:29)—as One who commanded a spiritual reality they deeply desired but struggled to grasp. Their minds were so set to think in terms of religious duty that they nearly missed the greatest opportunity for *relationship* in each of their lives. How often we do the same! Rather than step out in faith, we, like the Samaritan woman, first seek clarification. Her mind, like ours, asks for more information—more proof. Does Jesus answer her? Yes and no.

Jesus does not respond to her mind, but He does respond to her heart. He denies the natural man's request for explanation and challenges the inner man for faith. Rather than speak to her perceived need of understanding, he addresses her heart's need for healing. Thus, when she implicitly asks, "Are you greater than what I have experienced of life and God to this point?" Jesus pinpoints the nagging thirst within her which itself acknowledges that those resources have not been enough. In the midst of a beautiful invitation to accept living water, Jesus highlights the first of several obstacles that inhibit us from receiving the restorative work of God in our life: the well of hindrance, also known as the well of self.

To understand this concept more fully, let us turn to Genesis 37:1–24, the story of Joseph. As mentioned previously, the Samaritan woman's story takes place at Jacob's well, which was part of Joseph's inheritance. I daresay it is not by chance that Joseph, like the Samaritan woman many years later, had life-changing "well experiences."

Genesis 37 recounts the early part of Joseph's life—how he was favored by his father and hated by his brothers, and how he received two prophetic dreams that further aggravated this family rift. As a result, Joseph's brothers attacked him in the fields one day and threw him into a cistern, which is a type of well. Later, they took him out and sold him to some passing Ishmaelites, who eventually sold him to the Egyptian officer Potiphar.

During the early period of Joseph's life, the favor and anointing of God were apparent in his life. Possibly this added to Jacob's favoritism, for the Word says, referring to the two dreams, that Jacob "kept the matter in mind" (Gn 37:10). Joseph was blessed, but he was also prideful and foolish. A close study of his conversations with his father and brothers reveals that Joseph, like the woman at the well, was drawing largely from the "well of self" at this point in his walk with the Lord. Specifically, he was relying more on his own resources (natural gifts like intellect, talent, and position), than on God. He was chosen, but he had a lot to learn.

Thus, the heavenly Father, who weighs all things in his hands including the heart of man (Prv 21:2; 24:12), allowed some very harsh circumstances to pass through Joseph's life. Figuratively speaking, He allowed Joseph to be thrown into his "well of self" in order to drain this inhibiting resource from Joseph's life.

Joseph's first "dunking" was fairly mild. We soon find him in Genesis 39 successfully reigning over Potiphar's house. However, as again evidenced by his words when speaking to Potiphar's wife (v. 8–9), Joseph still attributes much of the credit for his success to himself. Though anointed and favored of God, Joseph still relies more on his own abilities than on God. As a result, God sends him back to the well (v. 20–21). Verse 21 states that Joseph was sent to the dungeon, the place "where the king's prisoners were kept." In ancient times, dried-up cisterns or wells, particularly those located near the palace, were often used for prisons. The Hebrew word for dungeon in verse 21 is the word *bowr* (pronounced bore), which means "cistern or well." The imagery is powerful—Joseph fails the test and is sent back for many more years in the well.

During this time, the Lord's favor and anointing remain with Joseph, and a great change takes place in Joseph's heart. When we hear from him again in Genesis 41:14–16, he is no longer the same man. Rather than prideful or self-reliant, he is humble, teachable, and aware of his own limitations. He is no longer drawing from the well of self but wholly dependent upon the springs of the living God (v. 16). In short, he has been restored, and he is ready to be used.

In Jeremiah 2:13, the Lord issues a judgment upon Israel saying, "My people have committed two sins: They have forsaken me, the spring of living water, and have dug their own cisterns, broken cisterns that cannot hold water." Remember that a cistern is a type of well, but actually it is less useful than a well. While a well is cut deep into the ground such that it receives the seepage of groundwater, a cistern is merely a stone tank that collects rainfall and above ground runoff. Thus, the judgment of this passage suggests that God's people have not only forsaken the best of the best—the spring of living water—but they also have attempted to provide for themselves by means of the least of leasts, cisterns—broken ones at that! What an accurate picture of our own resources compared with God's!

When we return to the woman at the well story, we see that this woman, like Joseph, had a choice to make. Would she continue relying on that portion of God and life that she felt she could control—that measure of understanding that she could store away in the well of her mind and draw out as needed (knowing this pool would eventually run dry), or would she accept Christ's invitation to surrender and be restored. Likewise, we have the same choice—to live by our own finite resources (including whatever we know of God) or to live by God's limitless supply. The Holy Spirit is for us a spring of living water. However, to accept him means we must confront and surrender the contents of our well of self. We must sacrifice our own resources. Like the widow of Elijah's day, we must give up all we've got, down to the very last drop, before the spring of God's provision will be loosed in our hearts and lives (1 Kgs 17:10–16).

Why did Joseph have to endure nearly two decades of draining? Because the Lord knew Joseph's future, which included his becoming second in command over all of Egypt, the largest kingdom of the known world. Only by drawing solely upon God would Joseph be able to exercise the wisdom and authority necessary to govern such a vast empire.

Like Joseph, we are identified in the Bible as being "seated with Christ in the heavenly realms" (Eph 2:6). Our heritage is a heritage of spiritual authority and blessing. To understand, let alone exercise, such authority, we must be drawing solely upon God. We must be willing, like the Samaritan woman, to surrender our preconceived notions, our control, and cry out to God in our thirst. We must be willing to take a chance—a lifetime leap of faith—surrendering our wells for the springs of eternal life. As long as we are being satisfied by our own resources, we will never experience the fullness of intimacy with Jesus Christ. There is only one way to the Father, only one person who can meet all of our needs, only one source of the living water of eternal life—Jesus Christ.

God has prepared a certain territory within his kingdom for each of us to govern (Eph 1:11–12). Just as Joseph held the keys to the important places and centers of control within Egypt (Gn 41:56), the Lord desires to entrust us with spiritual keys to unlock important places in individuals' lives, beginning with our own. These are the keys, described in Matthew 16:19, by which we may bind and loose the things of heaven on earth. We will study these keys more in following chapters.

It is awe inspiring to contemplate the grace of a God who would be willing to share so much of his authority with us. But we know from his Word that the Lord deeply desires intimacy with us, and there is no greater intimacy than to work together toward a divine and glorious purpose—the salvation of those we love. The "keys to the kingdom" are keys that unlock burdened places in human hearts: important spiritual power centers that the enemy has usurped and laid waste. These are the "ruined cities" and "places long devastated" of Isaiah 61:4. Christ is willing to give each of us a key ring, filled with unique opportunities to unlock the lives and hearts of people around us—to release captives, to open blind eyes, to lead the lame in walking, and to release the kingdom power of God in those individuals. After all, the kingdom of God dwells in the hearts of men and women (Lk 17:20–21).

For additional study, I ask you to consider the difference between the well of self and the springs of God's living water as they apply personally to your life. I have suggested that you search your soul to identify the contents of your well and the circumstances (both past and present) that tempt you to rely on yourself rather than God. Finally, I have asked you to prayerfully consider surrendering your well of self and inviting the Lord to do whatever it takes, as long as it takes, to establish in your life the fullness of spiritual heritage as we have in Jesus Christ.* To experience restoration, we must stop living solely in the natural and learn to operate also in the spiritual. We must "come of age" spiritually and take up our inheritance. It is time that we stop living in the past and allow the Lord to restore us for the future. We are women of God, not plunder (Jer 2:14). We are his helpmates, a holy bride, a royal priesthood. The choice is ours—where shall we draw and drink?

---

*If you are conducting this study in a small group, I recommend that the leader supply each woman with a rock and an inexpensive dangling key, either on a necklace or bracelet. Have each individual pray over her rock (representing the well of self) and then throw it away to some irretrievable place to seal her commitment. Also, have each woman wear the key (representing spiritual heritage) for a week or so. If you are doing this study alone, you may do the same for yourself. As the key dangles about your neck or wrist, let it serve as a reminder to pray for and seek a more complete understanding of our spiritual heritage in Christ.

Scripture Study

Read John 4:4–15.

1. What is the invitation Jesus gives to the Samaritan woman? What is the challenge? Does the woman accept this challenge? How do you know?

2. When the woman says, "You have nothing to draw with and the well is deep," who is she describing? How can this assessment be applied to nonbelievers? Christians?

Read Genesis 37:1–24.

1. Have you ever had "well" experiences like this? What did you learn about yourself? What did you learn about God?

2. What was the purpose of these experiences in Joseph's life? How did they prepare him for his destiny? *(see* Gn 41–45)

3. How does that compare to our spiritual destiny? What can we learn from Joseph's life about the sovereignty of God over our circumstances? How can this help us deal with the past?

Read Jeremiah 2:13–14.

1. What are the two charges the Lord issues against his people?

2. What do the cisterns represent?

Look up the following Scriptures: Isaiah 44:3 and 58:11–12; John 7:37–40; Revelations 21:6–7 and 22:1–17.

1. In your own words, explain the significance of water in these passages.

2. Who is the spring of living water?

3. What does it mean to have "living water" flowing in your life? What are the "signs" that testify to this flow?

Read 1 Kings 17:10–16.

1. How was the widow's oil a type of spring?

2. What does this story tell us about how such springs may be released in our lives?

3. What in your life right now might be compared to, or needs to become like, the widow's oil?

Reflection

In your journal, reflect on the following prompts:

1. List those things that make up your "well of self."

2. Identify the circumstances in your life through which you have learned the difference between relying on your resources rather than on God's.

3. What are the warning signs in your life that you are drawing from the well of self?

4. As you feel led, write out a prayer of surrender to God—surrendering the contents of your well in exchange for his springs, and committing to allow Him to teach you the fullness of the heritage you have in Jesus Christ.

Embracing the Past
through Forgiveness

5

The first issue raised by the woman at the well is one that many of us have struggled with: whether or not God will explain himself to us and provide us with a waterproof rationale for both the successes and shortcomings of life as we have experienced it. Something within us as humans simply has to know. We crave understanding. More aptly, we crave control.

In our society, knowledge equals power. Even with God, understanding provides some sense of security and predictability. We want to see God's plan before we take our first step of faith. We want the power of a completed calculation. "Okay, God, if I do this—then what will You do? If I yield here, then what will You ask of me next? Just what are You after, God? Just what are You about? Who are You?"

Certainly, God understands such questions. After all, we have been raised in a fallen world replete with hidden agendas, broken promises, and wasted heros. Most of us have had a fair share of disappointment in our lives—in people, various institutions, and unfulfilled dreams. God understands our hurt and suspicion. He sympathizes with our pain (Mt 9:36). In fact, He understands it so well that He has designed a plan for our healing.

This plan involves many facets, which we will study in the next several lessons. The first facet, or step, was presented in the previous chapter: accepting the invitation of Christ. The first and foremost step toward restoration involves surrendering personal effort (and intellect) and casting our all upon the promise of Jesus Christ. Oswald Chambers describes this experience in the "Discipline of Loneliness" as follows: "You must abandon all and fling yourself on God as a mere conscious being, and, seeking you'll find him. That teaching that presents consecration as giving to God our gifts, our possessions, our comrades is a profound error. These are all abandoned, and we give up forever our right to ourselves" (Lambert, p. 24).

When Jesus offers the Samaritan woman the living water of eternal, spiritual life, He presents her with a great challenge: to go beyond natural intellect and abilities, past and present experiences, and to set aside whatever her social or religious upbringing had prepared her to accept as "God." In short, He leaves it up to her to decide, "Am I greater than Jacob? Are you willing to take a leap of faith and see for yourself?"

Before we continue, remember that Jesus's invitation involved more than salvation. As we see from John 4:25, the Samaritan woman already believed in Messiah. In fact, her faith in Messiah may well have been the only remaining lifeline that kept her afloat. Because of this, her story is more than a story of a "salvation" experience. Rather than salvation, the crucial issue in the opening scene at the well centers upon faith. Many people have professed faith in God for salvation, but what about intimacy with God? What about complete restoration in this life, as well as the next? Many of us can believe in a God who will keep us from hell, but how many of us know the God who cares intimately for our every thought and who desires to bless our lives more than we can ask or think (Eph 3:20)? How many of us, if we are truly honest with ourselves, have the faith to believe God is uncompromising in his goodness, despite all the seemingly contrary "natural" evidence? How many of us have the faith to surrender ourselves from this moment forward, fully into the hands of Jesus Christ, not just for salvation but for complete restoration and healing, regardless of what it takes to get there? After all, the process of moving from "well" to "spring" isn't always pretty; there may be a lot of mud and mire to deal with along the way (Ps 40:1–3).

Nonetheless, the first step requires our complete surrender. By faith, we must accept the Lord's invitation, first for salvation and, secondly, for complete restoration and healing. We must abandon our broken cisterns (Jer 2:13) and embrace the springs of living water that flow from Christ alone.

The second facet, or step, of restoration involves forgiveness. There is simply no way around this issue. No matter how abusive or bleak our pasts have been, forgiveness *is* the key to overcoming them. If you can imagine it, forgiveness dangles from our wrists as one of several "keys" as discussed in the last chapter (Mt 16:19). Next to the others, the key of forgiveness may seem rather dull, even awkward and unattractive. Yet it is one of the most important keys on the whole ring. It literally unlocks the past, removing mountains of painful memories and casting them into the sea (along with all the sins that God has forgiven mankind) (Mt 21:21; Mi 7:19).

For this reason and others, which we shall see momentarily, Jesus takes a seemingly abrupt detour in his dialogue with the Samaritan woman. In John 4:15, the woman replies, "Sir, give me this water so that I won't get thirsty and have to keep coming here to draw water." By "here," the woman refers to more than the physical site of Jacob's well. "Here" also refers to the emotional pain and spiritual longing that have driven her from one relationship to the next throughout her life. In a moment of life-changing epiphany, her spirit cries out, "Jesus, save me!" (Mt 14:28-31).

The Master replies, "Go call your husband" (v. 16). As we know from the story, the woman declares she has no husband, and Jesus confirms her response. In verse 18, He elaborates: "The fact is, you have had five husbands, and the man you now have is not your husband. What you have just said is quite true."

"Sir," the woman said, "I can see that you are a prophet" (v. 19).

Now there is an element of humor amidst all this conversing about husbands. After all, how would you feel if God Incarnate showed up at the grocery store one day and spilled the nitty-gritty beans of your past? The fact that the woman came up with any response is commendable. I think I might have stood there speechless or looked for some hole to crawl into. She doesn't. Instead, she replies honestly and humbly (and perhaps just a little sarcastically) to this stranger's forthright account of her shortcomings—"I can see that you are a prophet."

Whatever the nature of her response, she doesn't run. She confirms her acceptance of Christ's promise by allowing him to begin the delicate surgery of removing her old self. Like any good surgeon, Jesus goes straight for the heart. He secures the most vital organ first, knowing that others will follow in time.

Why does Jesus tell her to call her husband? He does so for the same reason that God told both Hagar and Elijah to "Go back" (Gen 16:9–10; 1 Kgs 19:15–18). Simply stated, we cannot enter into new relationships or seasons of life until we have been rightly released from the past. When God calls us to go back (whether figuratively or literally) and face those who have injured us, He has a definite purpose in mind. To understand that purpose, let's explore the text in John 4 more closely.

Jesus stated that the woman had had five husbands and was now living with a sixth man. We are not told why she divorced or, more properly, was divorced from these men (since women could not initiate divorce in those times). Perhaps some of them died (which in those days was believed to be a sign of Divine disapproval). Perhaps the woman couldn't bear children. We don't know why the men divorced her, and I don't suppose it really matters. The bottom line is that this woman had experienced great misfortune and rejection in her life.

Now she was living with a man, unmarried and, therefore, subject to both public and religious scorn. Scholars suspect she was not married at the time of her encounter because either the sixth man refused to marry her or her fifth husband had not divorced her properly, leaving her unable to marry. In either case, her situation was grave. Marriage amounted to everything for women in those times. Unable to own property and with no education, women had little hope for financially supporting themselves. They needed the protection of a husband.

Throughout Scripture, the relationship between a husband and wife is compared with Christ's relationship with the Church (Jer 3:12–14; Is 54:4–7). Both individually and corporately, we are called to the close communion of marital intimacy with Jesus Christ. We are each his Bride (Is 62:5; Rv 19:7; 21:9–10). First Corinthians 13:12 states that, when Christ returns, we shall know him fully even as we are fully known. Jesus desires our intimacy. He desires to be wed with us through worship as our spiritual husband.

The goal of Jesus's command to the Samaritan woman, "Go call your husband," was not to shame or hurt her. Rather, the Lord intended to set her free from the rejection and pain of these past relationships. Furthermore, He sought to prepare her to enter into a new covenant relationship with him. By reconciling the issues of her past, she could be cleansed and purified—renewed as a Bride "without spot or wrinkle" (Eph 5:27). Then, and only then, would she be ready to enter fully into the most important marriage of her life—marriage to the Lamb of God.

In John 4:21, Jesus addresses the woman directly. In many translations, the term used in this passage is rendered merely as "woman." However, in the original language, the term that Jesus uses suggests great intimacy. Literally translated, this term, *gunee*, means "wife." Look again at the number of "husbands" to which the Samaritan woman had previously been wed—five legal marriages plus one common law relationship. For all practical purposes, the Samaritan woman had been married six times to six different husbands. Jesus becomes her seventh, a number that in the Bible signifies wholeness. Despite the failure of her youthful marriages, she finds completion in Christ. So it is with us.

Whether we have had as many literal marriages as the Samaritan woman or not, we can all relate to past experiences whereby we have wed ourselves to various individuals and things apart from God. Such relationships served as *idols* of security and significance to help us cope with certain seasons of our lives. These relationships may or may not have been sexual. The important thing is that we placed our trust in people, things—and even ideas—rather than God. Most likely, we found ourselves sadly disappointed. We may have felt used, deceived, or just plain stupid for putting ourselves in such vulnerable positions. In some of those relatioships, we may not have had a conscious choice. It may be that while still children we were "sold out" to ideologies and circumstances that opposed the truth of God in our lives. In essence, we were deceived (Gn 3:13).

Whatever the case, these experiences represent "binding relationships" that, if not properly broken, inhibit our maturity in Christ. We can only grow in intimacy with God to the extent that we are able to grow with others. First John 2–4 deals extensively with this concept; in verses 20–21 of Chapter 4, the Word says "If anyone says, 'I love God,' yet hates his brother, he is a liar. For anyone who does not love his brother, whom he has seen, cannot love God, whom he has not seen. And He has given us this command: Whoever loves God must also love his brother."

Again, God doesn't say these things to shame or hurt us. He is not out to set the greatest possible stumbling block in our paths toward him. Rather, the Lord emphasizes a basic spiritual truth. Our intimacy with God corresponds to our intimacy with one another, and vice versa. We may only hope to understand and love God to the extent that we have understood and loved one another. Likewise, we are only able to love one another to the extent we have experienced the transforming love of God.

Thus, if there are outstanding issues from broken relationships in our lives, these will necessarily inhibit us from drawing closer to God. So it was with the woman at the well. How could she hope to draw near to Christ in the intimacy of worship (which means "to kiss"), if all her past experiences of intimacy had only ended in rejection, which left scars of unmet needs, unhealed hurts, and fear of repetition? Similarly, how can we hope to love God if our hearts are still bleeding from past wounds of those who claimed to, or should have, "loved" us? These issues must be resolved; we must be released from them before we can fully enter into new phases of life. No wonder then that Jesus said, "Go, call your husband…"

The wounds of past relationships can hold tremendous influence over us if they are not properly healed. Many of us today walk around wielding heavy chains to the past—often to specific people or experiences of which we have not let go. There are many teachings on spiritual bondage and the methods, including forgiveness, by which such bondage may be broken. It is not my desire to contradict or nullify any of these other biblically sound teachings. Furthermore, I do not believe the method expressed here is *the truth* that excludes or supersedes all else. Simply for the purpose of discussion, I have compiled the following elaboration of how we may have become bound to, and now may become released from, past "binding relationships."

There are four main ways we may be bound to past relationships: unforgiveness; unhealed hurts or needs; wrong habits or thinking patterns; and natural debt or unbroken contracts.

For the remainder of this lesson, we will discuss only the first type of bondage: *unforgiveness*. Then, in the next lesson, we will study the remaining three.

By far, the majority of our bondage to the past results from unforgiveness. This is due, in part, to a tremendous lack of understanding within the Body of Christ regarding what true forgiveness is and what it isn't. The word "forgive" first appears in the Bible in Genesis 50:17. Upon their father's death, the sons of Jacob feared that their brother Joseph (whom we studied in the last chapter) would seek retaliation for all the wrongs they had done to him. This was a reasonable fear, since Joseph, at that time, had the power in Egypt to completely obliterate the tribes of Israel if he had wished. Realizing this potential, Joseph's brothers sent him a message saying: "I ask you to *forgive* your brothers the sins and the wrongs they committed in treating you so badly. Now please *forgive* the sins of the servants of the God of your father" (Gn 50:17).

The last part of verse 17 states, "When their message came to him, Joseph wept." The remainder of this story offers us a wealth of information on the reality of what true forgiveness involves. Joseph wept when he received his brothers' request for forgiveness. I believe he wept for two reasons: He wept as he recalled the pain of his past and all the harsh circumstances through which God had delivered him. He also wept that his brothers would fear his harm, not knowing the overwhelming love he felt for each one of them.

In verse 18, the brothers throw themselves down at his feet and offer to become his slaves. Joseph replies, "Don't be afraid. Am I in the place of God? You intended to harm me, but God intended it for good to accomplish what is now being done, the saving of many lives" (v. 19–20).

In his reply, Joseph acknowledges three essential truths that define biblical forgiveness. The first truth of biblical forgiveness identifies that we are not in the place of God. No matter what has happened to us, no matter how badly a person has wronged us, we do not have the right to judge that individual. Why? Because we haven't a clue as to what the "big picture" really looks like. We do not know what was done to that person, or to the person before him that may have prompted (though not excused) his or her behavior. As Liberty Savard states in *Shattering Your Strongholds,* "How many generations back do you want to go to before you think you can finally place blame on the original perpetrator? The key lies not in finding where to place the blame, but in releasing … your pain so that God can make you whole" (Bridge-Logos, 1997, p. xiii).

Fault-finding is a trap. It represents the antithesis of forgiveness, and it will never produce healing. The Bible is clear: There is a Judge, but we are not *him* (Acts 10:42). God alone knows the hearts of men (1 Sm 16:7) and can execute just judgments which He will do in his time and his way. For us to forgive, we must have faith in God that He will take up our offenses and make every situation right on the grand scale of eternal punishments and rewards (Rom 12:19). Until then, we must humbly accept that there is much to life and human nature we simply do not understand.

The second truth of biblical forgiveness involves the certainty of God's sovereignty over our lives. In Genesis 50:20, Joseph tells his brothers, "You intended to harm me, but God intended it for good to accomplish what is now being done, the saving of many lives." In this statement, Joseph acknowledged the sovereignty of God over all his circumstances. In doing so, he did not dismiss or make light of the difficulty of those hard times; rather he claimed the eternal purpose that those events played in the working out of God's will. Romans 8:28 contains one of the most beautiful promises in all of Scripture: "And we *know* that God causes *all things* to work together for *good* to those who love God, to those who are called according to *His* purpose" (NASB, emphasis added). It does not matter what evils we have done or have been done to us; God will turn any or all of it around for good if we will release ourselves to him through surrender and forgiveness.

Finally, the third truth of biblical forgiveness involves blessing one's enemies. In Genesis 50:21, Joseph tells his brothers, "So therefore, do not be afraid. I will provide for you and your little ones. So he comforted them and spoke kindly to them." Instead of giving his brothers what they deserved, Joseph (serving as a prototype for Christ) blesses them and provides for them. Matthew 5:44 records the words of Jesus when He says, "But I say to you, love your enemies and pray for those who persecute you … " Why does Jesus say this? Verse 45 states the reason, "so that you may be sons of your Father who is in heaven; for He causes his sun to rise on the evil and the good, and sends rain on the righteous and the unrighteous." God has given us a standard to follow in our forgiveness, that of amazing grace, the same grace by which we ourselves have been saved and sanctified.

Now before we become angry or frustrated by the seeming impossibility of meeting such a high standard, we must remember: We are not doing this on our own. God has not called us to do what He has not already done for us, in us, and through us. Philippians 2:13 states "for it is God who is at work in you, both to *will* and to *work* for his good pleasure." We are not in this thing alone. God will help us to forgive even the most heinous crimes. All we have to do is trust Him.

All three truths of biblical forgiveness that we have studied from Genesis boil down to this: Forgiveness requires faith. When all the circumstances and individual memories are stripped away, the choice to forgive remains one between you and God. Do you trust God enough to let go of the past? Do you believe He is big enough to heal you and take care of the other guy in whatever way seems best to God? Do you love him enough to let it go?

Several months ago I faced a need to forgive someone who had recently hurt me. In the midst of glorious prayer time, I saw a vision of myself standing outside an open door. Inside, I could sense a greater Presence of the Lord than anything I had ever before known. Everything within me longed to enter into that intimacy. I started to go through the door, but I couldn't. On my back were strapped several large parcels, and they prevented me from being able to fit through the door frame. Just then, the Holy Spirit appeared and said, "You may enter in, but not with all that." He motioned to my baggage. I knew it represented the grudges I was harboring against this person. The Spirit continued, "If you seek intimacy—true intimacy—with God, you must not let anything stand in the way." I had no trouble letting go of my unforgiveness that day. When compared with the awesome splendor of knowing Christ, unforgiveness seemed like worthless garbage.

Biblical forgiveness in no way suggests ignoring or dismissing a wrong word or action. Rather it transfers responsibility from an unable party to an able One. The Hebrew word for forgive is *nasa* which means "to lift." Thus, forgiveness means lifting the yoke of responsibility for recompense and placing it upon the Cross, where Jesus "was crushed for our iniquities" and purchased our healing (Is 53:5). The parable of the unmerciful servant powerfully illustrates this transaction (Mt 18:23–35). What the unmerciful servant failed to learn was that, if God were big enough to "pay off" the servant's own immense debt, He could also have paid off his brother's minor debt. (I am not suggesting a complete release of liability in all cases. In circumstances involving ongoing sexual or physical abuse, the offender must be stopped. The Bible clearly teaches we are to submit to civil authorities and laws (Rom 13:1–3). Thus, the "lifting" here discussed refers primarily to emotional and spiritual debts that God alone can restore.)

The hardest part of forgiveness occurs in the interim between the time we must choose to obey the Lord by forgiving and when, as a result of our forgiveness, we begin to experience God's replenishing of that from which we were robbed. Matthew 7:2 assures us whatever measure we give out will be given back to us. When we forgive those who have wronged us, God promises to restore whatever we lost by "lifting" that debt. In short, when we forgive, God assumes the loan, and He always pays back in full (Jn 10:10).

Biblical forgiveness amounts to a spiritual transaction whereby we agree to release our grudges to God, trusting that He is able to restore all things in perfect justice. We may not see the fullness of that restoration in this life, but we know it will come. We trust our debts to him—both those we have received from others and those we have amassed ourselves.

Before we leave this point, I remind you that there are serious consequences to unforgiveness. The Bible says that those who harbor unforgiveness will be turned over to "tormentors" (Mt 18:34). Such torment may result in sickness, financial ruin, broken relationships, and disabled spiritual growth. Jesus himself stated that we will be forgiven as we forgive others (Mt 6:14–15). The implication stands that, if we fail to lift the debts off our brothers, God will not lift ours. He will allow us to feel the weight of our own sinful natures in order to teach us compassion for the sinful natures of others.

All in all, forgiveness represents a divine privilege and blessing. It is a privilege to release others from the captivity of sin's debt, and that is what we do each time we forgive another's sin. We participate, on a smaller scale, in the divine role of Christ on the Cross. We assume another's guilt and take it to God, who miraculously makes all things beautiful in their time (Eccl 3:11). As we exercise this priestly role, we find ourselves ironically blessed. What looked like loss becomes great gain, for the Lord honors our mercy with double portions of his own. We may not receive an exact return of whatever physical, emotional, or spiritual inventory we lost in our relationship with the abuser, but we will nonetheless receive a gracious return in our lives. In the end, we are the ones most blessed when we choose to forgive.

When Jesus asks the woman at the well to "Go call your husband," He initiates a process of forgiveness through which she may be set free from her past. We know there must have been more to their discussion, because she later tells the villagers, "Come, see a man who told me everything I ever did" (Jn 4:29). If we desire restoration—even revival—in our lives, we should anticipate the Lord's direction to call up whatever issues in our past have not been resolved. In order for us to be able to enter in fully to the intimacy which Jesus desires with us, we must be rightly released from all past relationships. The only way to begin that process is through forgiveness.

Scripture Study

Read John 4: 15-19. Answer the following questions:

1. Why does Jesus tell the woman, "Go call your husband"? How does she reply?

2. What does a husband symbolize in the natural? In the spiritual? (*see* Jer 3:12–14 and Is 54:4–7)

3. How can Jesus's direction to the Samaritan woman be compared to the Lord's command to Hagar in Genesis 16:9–10?

4. Why is it important that we deal with our past and, specifically, past relationships with others?

5. What is Jesus's goal in this portion of his conversation with the Samaritan woman?

Turn to Genesis 50:15–21. This passage includes the first mention of the word "forgive" in the Bible. It relates the later half of Joseph's life (which we studied in lesson 4).

1. What is taking place in this passage?

2. What do Joseph's brothers fear?

3. How does Joseph respond to their plea?

4. What three "truths" of forgiveness does Joseph's response illustrate?

Read Matthew 18:23–35.

1. What does the wicked servant fail to learn? What is his punishment?

2. Who or what do the "tormentors" represent?

3. Is God serious about forgiveness?

Read 1 Peter 2:23-24; Matthew 5:44-45; and Luke 6:35.
These Scriptures provide us with a justification for God's high standard of forgiveness.
1. What is that justification?

2. What example has God set for us? Why?

3. What does this suggest about God's character?

Finally, read Genesis 9:20–29.
1. How does Ham's response to his father's sin differ from the responses of the other two sons?

2. How can Shem and Japheth's "covering" be seen as an act of forgiveness or grace?

3. What precedent do they provide for us?

4. How does Noah respond?

5. What does this suggest about the role of forgiveness in blessing?

Reflection

Make a list of those past relationships to which you currently feel "bound." (Hint: If there is pain associated with the memory of that person or circumstance, you are probably still bound in some fashion.) Make note of those that stand out as bondages of unforgiveness. Using the following prayer, choose to forgive these individuals, and ask the Lord to begin healing you by restoring all that was lost through this person's debt.

Forgiveness Prayer

> *Father, I thank You for the divine privilege of forgiveness. I declare that You alone are the Judge of mankind. I do not see as You see, and I may not understand why _____ (name of person) treated me in this way. However, I choose to turn this debt over to You. I forgive _____ (name of person) for _____ (state offense—be as specific as you need to). I forgive him/her for robbing me of my confidence and worth. I choose by Your grace to forgive and I declare that this offense may never again be used against him/her. And Lord, I ask You now to heal me of all that I lost through these circumstances. Restore my physical, emotional, and spiritual heritage. Give me a right understanding of who I am in you. Thank You for the certainty of Your complete justice and mercy both for me, for those who have wronged me, and for those I have wronged. In Jesus's name, Amen. (Repeat individually for each offender).*

Note: Sometimes we may need to forgive ourselves for any bad choices we made that hurt us. It is often much easier to forgive others than to forgive ourselves. As you feel led, you may wish to end your prayer session by stating your forgiveness of yourself. In the same vein, we may have encountered circumstances in our lives for which we need to "forgive" God. Obviously, since God is without sin, He does not need to be forgiven. However, if our lack of understanding at the time made us feel hurt or disappointed by God, praying through forgiveness may help us overcome any reservation or mistrust we may feel towards God as a result of those circumstances. For example, if you experienced the death of a parent during childhood, you may still harbor unresolved feelings of hurt toward God for not protecting you from those circumstances. As an adult, you may still hold back something of yourself from God in fear that He will not protect you (like He "failed" to then). Praying through forgiveness to God will help cleanse those deeply embedded wounds and allow for the replenishing of your lost trust.

If at any time you feel overburdened by your need to forgive or just need someone to share these struggles, please contact your class leader, pastor, Christian counselor, or trustworthy Christian friend. The Bible states that as we "confess our sins to one another" we will be healed (Jas 5:16).

Breaking the Contract

6

In the last lesson, we began to study how to be freed from the past. Forgiveness represents the first and foremost key to open that door. It matters not whether our offenders deserve to be forgiven. We forgive for our own sakes to obey God's law and to receive his healing. We entrust our debts, and debtors, to his eternal care. If we really desire to know God more intimately, we must break our ties to the past, and the primary way to do that is through forgiveness.

Since completing the last lesson and praying the forgiveness prayer, the Holy Spirit likely prompted you to forgive someone—maybe many people. You may have even been surprised at names and circumstances that came to mind requiring your forgiveness. When you first learn about the process of forgiveness, it is not uncommon to discover that the Lord brings up many circumstances from the past for forgiveness and healing—sometimes going all the way back to childhood. I encourage you not to dismiss or try to explain away these promptings. No matter how silly they may seem, pray these situations through and speak forgiveness for every individual involved. It may not seem like much is happening, but in the spirit realm many ties are being broken—unhealthy bonds that add up and inhibit potential in our lives with Christ. Let the Lord have his way and enjoy the new sense of freedom and joy that will follow your submission to this spiritual makeover.

In this lesson we will be looking at three other ways that we may be tied to our past, besides unforgiveness. These include natural debt or unbroken contracts, unhealed hurts, and wrong habits or thinking patterns.

First, let's look at debt. In both the Old and New Testaments, the Bible repeatedly admonishes believers to stay out of debt. Romans 13:8 states that believers are to "let no debt remain outstanding," and Deuteronomy 15:6 promises that "you shall lend to many nations but will borrow from none." Peter declares in 1 Peter 2:19–20 that there is no glory in suffering for wrongdoing, of which debt is a frequent contributor. Natural debt and unbroken legal contracts can and do affect the spiritual health of believers. This should not surprise us. After all, look at how the world responds to these legal masters. Outstanding debt can produce lethal amounts of stress on both relationships and individuals. It represents a key contributor to many different health problems and marital strife. Financial debt involves both natural and spiritual bondage, which significantly affects believers' lives.

In Matthew 6:24, Jesus plainly states that man cannot serve two masters. He declares "Either he will hate the one and love the other, or he will be devoted to the one and despise the other. You cannot serve both God and Money." Debt in the natural correlates to spiritual enslavement. Whomever or whatever you owe, to some extent that person or thing owns you until you have paid off the debt or otherwise obtained a legal or spiritual release from those circumstances. God does not view debt lightly, and neither should we. As a just judge, He will hold us responsible for our actions (Rom 14:12). Therefore, with the same vigilance by which we pursue spiritual freedom, we should purpose to seek the "natural" freedom of living debt-free (Rom 13:8).

In the same vein, unbroken contracts, (including vows and covenants), whether business or personal, may represent a second type of "natural" link to the past. Not all of these contracts are bad, only those that may have been formed outside or even in opposition to God's will for our lives. The Bible states in 2 Corinthians 6:14 that believers are not to be yoked together with unbelievers, "For what fellowship can light have with darkness?" The only exception to this rule applies to marriages formed prior to conversion in which one person is a believer while the other is not. In those cases, Paul instructs the believer to remain with the unbeliever so long as the unbeliever is willing (1 Cor 7:12–17). All other contracts involving believers and nonbelievers should be viewed with extreme caution. We are to be "in" the world, but not "of" the world (Jn 17:14). The distinction lies in the attitude of our heart regarding why we would desire to enter or remain in that contract and/or debt. As Paul states in Romans 13:8, the only acceptable debt in believers' lives is that of love.

Obtaining a "right release" from contractual agreements we have made, or covenants we have established, may take time. Certainly, I would not recommend knee-jerk reactions. If you feel there are agreements you have made that are binding you in a spiritually unhealthy fashion, you should seek the Lord for his guidance. Ecclesiastes 8:6 states: "For there is a proper time and procedure for every matter, though a man's misery weighs heavily upon him." The Holy Spirit will give you the proper procedure and timing to cleanse your life of unholy influences. Realize, however, that you may experience a season of reaping what you have sown before your life is entirely set in order. A diligent heart that truly desires God's best will persevere and humbly accept the path of righteousness that God ordains (Ps 23:3).

Thus, unforgiveness, and natural debt or unbroken contracts, represent two of four primary ways we may be bound to relationships in our past. A third bondage results from unhealed hurts or needs. Like unforgiveness, these bondages may prove significant both in number and size. Such links may be intertwined with issues of unforgiveness, as we often struggle to forgive those who have deeply wounded us. In other words, these strongholds may involve many layers extending back to childhood. Many of these issues center upon those in various "caregiver" roles who helped us form, by intent or neglect, our expectations of the adult relationships we are now experiencing, including our relationship with God. Deciphering these complex patterns and the unhealed hurts or needs that lie at their root can provide great insight into our current expectations and experiences of others. Furthermore, by identifying our unhealed hurts and needs, we open the door for God's healing. Once again, we exercise our spiritual "keys" to unlock human hearts, beginning with our own, in order to release those burdens and relationships to the Lord. As we cooperate with him, the Holy Spirit will reveal in prayer the areas of our hearts that need to be restored. He will show us exact instances when wounds were received and the hurtful judgments we may have formed that keep us bound to past pain. We then surrender these areas to him through prayer and receive his truth. Jesus said in John 8:32, "You shall know the truth and the truth shall make you free."

Our obedience to confront what the Spirit unveils allows God to initiate a process of inner healing and deliverance that enables us to mature in him. Wholeness comes as we partner with him, following his lead in our transformation.

Finally, a fourth way we may be bound to the past is through wrong behaviors and thinking patterns. These include any forms of response, whether overt (i.e., drug or food addictions, sexual impurity, gossip) or subtle (i.e., judgmental thoughts, resistance to the Holy Spirit) which contradict the truth of God's word. For example, we may reject a certain teaching on tithing simply because of a wrong suspicion that God desires to "take" from us. The Bible declares that God owns the cattle on a thousand hills and has no need of human assistance (Ps 50:10–12). Furthermore, God promises in his Word to provide all of our needs (Phil 4:19). The picture is clear: God is a giver, not a taker. However, because of certain past experiences, we may have adopted a wrong view of God that prompts us to respond inappropriately when the right circumstances play out (Savard, p. 5).

Wrong thinking and behavior patterns rob Christians of peace and joy by causing us to run from the very hands of those through whom God would bless us most, including himself. Such strongholds blind us to the truth and inhibit our growth in God. Often, they become crutches we cling to rather than seek the Lord's healing. Because many of them have been with us a long time, we find them more comfortable than the risk of intimate exposure. However, God cannot heal what we refuse to let him have. Thus, as we seek to experience more fully what it means to be "married" to God, the Holy Spirit will begin to reveal the ways, however subtle, in which our thoughts and behaviors do not line up with God's will. As I mentioned in Lesson 1, his process of revelation and renewal is called *sanctification*—being set apart for God (Acts, 26:18; 1 Cor 6:11), and represents a crucial aspect of true salvation.

When Jesus asks the woman at the well to "Go call her husband," He is interested in more than the men of her past life. He desires to bring release and healing, through forgiveness, for all the unhealed hurts and unmet needs associated with those relationships. He purposes to break the bondage of her rejection and realign her mistaken notions of God and worship (as seen in John 4:20–26). In short, Jesus wants to set her free just like He wants to set us free. Doing so may require a painful look into the past, but only for a moment. After all, no matter how grim our pasts may have been, no matter how many times we, like the Samaritan woman, may have been rejected, today is a new day in the Lord. As Isaiah 2:4–5 states: "No longer will they call you Deserted, or name your land [heart] Desolate. But you will be called Hephzibah and your land Beulah; for the Lord will take delight in you and your land will be married. As a young man marries a maiden, so will your sons marry you; as a bridegroom rejoices over his bride, so will your God rejoice over you."

To better understand the exchange taking place between the Samaritan woman's past "husbands" and her new relationship with Christ, let's take a closer look at marital contracts in Jewish law. The terms "husband" and "wife" are legal terms describing two parties involved in what is ultimately a spiritual contract. In Romans 7:1–4, Paul uses marriage as an analogy for the whole law and what it means to live in bondage to the law. He explains that a woman is "bound" to her husband and can only be released from this marital obligation through his death. Paul then establishes a comparison between marital contracts and the whole law, claiming that we also can only be released from the "binding relationships" of sin through death. In other words, the only way out of binding relationships, in God's eyes, is through the death of one or both parties. There simply is no other way.

In the natural realm, mankind has concocted many loopholes for escaping the legal contracts that become displeasing to us, including marriage. However, in God's court, which exists in the spiritual realm and before which every man will someday have to give an account of his life (Rom 14:12), no such clauses are recognized. God's standard is clear—once you have entered a binding relationship (which entails both natural and spiritual connections), the only way out is death—period. That is distressing news—but not for the Christian. Romans 7:4–6 explains that through Christ's death we also died to our old selves and are thereby released from the law and all binding relationships that we entered into through sin. In Christ, we are new creations (2 Cor 5:17). By his blood, we are set free from the "binding relationships" of our lives whether those relationships involved other people (unforgiveness, unhealed hurts or needs) or things (wrong thinking/behavior patterns or debt, including unbroken, legal contracts).

Thus, when we find ourselves inhibited, or our intimacy with God somehow "blocked," by unbroken ties to the past, we need only to apply what Christ has already accomplished. Jesus has paid the price for our freedom: That is an incontestable fact. However, there may be times when we experience an attack of the enemy upon vulnerable, unfinished areas of our lives. In those instances, the devil may demand "proof" of our freedom.

At this point, some may ask "Wasn't all that taken care of when I became a Christian—a 'new creature' in Christ (2 Cor 5:17)?" Yes and no. Yes, when we become Christians, professing faith in Jesus as Lord and Savior, our names are transferred to the Lamb's Book of Life. The old passes away, and we are made new. All our sins are instantly atoned for and we are betrothed to the Lord. However, even though our life is stamped "Forgiven," much of the old junk will remain until we choose to apply the power of our new status in God.

For example, let's say you have rental property and some renters move in. After a while, they stop paying their rent, begin tearing up your property and heaping up a lot of junk in your life. You have every right as the landlord to kick them out. They have absolutely no right to stay. However, they will stay until you take the initiative to go before a judge and serve them an eviction notice. So it is with the enemy's hold on much of our lives. As Christians, we have every right to kick him out. He has no claim to any part of our lives. We have been set free from sin and all its bonds by the blood of Jesus. However, Satan will continue to rule over us in various areas of our thoughts and lives until we serve him the eviction notice of the Cross and claim our freedom as the Bride of Christ alone. Freedom, like divorce, doesn't just happen—it may require a hearing.

When Jesus asks the woman at the well to call her husband, He essentially asks her to acknowledge the binding relationships of her past. For us, those relationships may take the form of previous marriages (as in her situation) but they may also take many other forms, such as unhealthy allegiances to certain friendships, family members, possessions, events, habits, or even beliefs. Anything that consistently comes between us and God represents a "binding relationship," a giving of ourselves to something other than God.

These relationships cause us to shift our focus from God and his plan for our lives and become enmeshed in sin (unforgiveness, unhealed hurts or needs, wrong patterns of thinking/behavior, and natural debt). As a result, these relationships diminish our potential by inhibiting the work of God in and through our lives. By their nature, they are destructive. They damage our confidence, drain our strength, and steal our faith for tomorrow's good. Like the woman at the well, we become outcasts to the heavenly blessings of life in God. Like her, we stand on the outside looking in and wondering: How did I ever end up *here*? (Jn 4:15)

Fortunately, there is hope because our God is merciful (Jer 3:12). Jesus does not ask the woman at the well to call up her past in order to hurt or shame her. Rather, his design is much greater. In the closing scene of their dialogue (Jn 4:25–26), the woman professes a heartfelt faith that the Messiah would come and explain all things to her. In essence, she proclaims the one hope that has sustained her through all her pain—someday Messiah will come, and though everyone else in my life has abandoned me, He will receive me. Already this woman loved the Lord and had set her life on his acceptance. When Jesus responds, "I who speak to you am He" (v. 26), He receives her faith. He accepts her. In so doing, He takes her for his Bride. As seen from the following account of her witness to the town, Jesus removes the shame of her widowhood, her outcast status, by wedding her to himself in a profound act of grace (*see* Is 54:4–5), the same grace with which He chooses each of us.

A few final notes about the five husbands in this story:

First of all, there are actually six—five she married and one she lived with. This number is significant because Jesus becomes her seventh husband. In the Bible, the number seven implies completeness or wholeness. Jesus completes this broken woman by accepting her for his Bride, just as He accepts us.

The husbands symbolically represent those things to which we "wed" ourselves in the hope of finding security, identity, or fulfillment in both natural and spiritual realms. Some of these marriages may be "arranged marriages." Within the culture of that time, it is likely that her first and perhaps even second marriages were arranged by her parents. This suggests that the initial "marriages" or binding habits of our lives are often passed down to us from our families of origin. The Bible calls this the "sin of the fathers," which may be passed down as much as four generations (Ex 34:7). The Hebrew word for "sin" in this phrase suggests a weakness or character flaw. Thus, we often inherit character flaws or weaknesses from our families, which predispose us to mimic their mistakes.

As an example from my own life, my parents are both intellectuals. From childhood I was raised to believe that education and knowledge were of utmost importance in life. For lack of knowing better, my parents raised me up as a child bride to "marry" or "worship" intellectualism. Even after becoming a Christian, I still pursued this "lover" from my youth because I did not know any better. Until I fully separated myself from the thoughts and habits of that "binding relationship" through the blood of Jesus, I was unable to give myself fully to the Lord.

So it is with all of our previous "marriages"—we must be fully divorced (both in the natural and, more importantly, the spiritual realm of the heart) before we are able to give ourselves fully to our current relationship (whether that is to God or to a "natural" husband). There is good news: All of these relationships can be broken, nullified by the blood of Jesus (representing his atoning death and our identified death in him). Satan will continue to rule over us in various areas of our thoughts and lives until we serve him the eviction notice of the Cross and claim our freedom.

The prayer sequence for breaking binding relationships is simple: Begin by forgiving everyone involved, then repent of that relationship, asking God to forgive you. No matter how you got into that relationship, it was a sin in God's eyes, and you must take responsibility for allowing it to influence you. Repent means "to turn your back on" something (*Strong's*). By repenting of the relationship, you are "turning your back" on its binding influence. Ask the Lord, by his blood, to break all contracts you have formed through the relationship and release you from reaping any further destruction as a result of it (*see* Gal 6:7–8). Conclude by asking God to heal you and restore whatever may have been lost through that association.

Most importantly, remember that the Lord's purpose for asking the woman at the well to call her husband was so that she could be set free from the pain of those past relationships and sanctified ("set apart") for marriage to the Lord. God is abundantly merciful. He has no hidden agendas. He operates out of a love so pure most of us struggle to receive it. God wants to be our husband. He wants to provide for us a security, identity, and fulfillment that will never fade. As the Song of Solomon attests, the Lord is passionately in love with us, his Bride. He is a trustworthy husband in whom we can find eternal rest for our souls.

For study and reflection, I have asked you to spend some time looking up a few additional Scriptures that relate to the "marriage promises" of God. I have also asked you to prayerfully consider whatever binding relationships you may need to renounce in order to be set apart for God. If you have any questions or would like someone to pray with you, I encourage you to contact your class leader, pastor, Christian counselor, or trustworthy friend. This is the final chapter dealing with the past. While we will move on from here to the glorious union of worship, I challenge you to remain sensitive as the Holy Spirit continues to stir up issues that may need further reflection. The process of sanctification continues throughout our lives. There is no simple 1-2-3 to it, as you may be inclined to believe by the format of this study. The steps continue to inter-mingle, producing a continual inward, upward spiral of intimacy as we disengage from worldly relationships and embrace a heavenly union with God's heart.

Scripture Study

Read Genesis 32. In this story, Jacob wrestles with God on the night before he returns home to face his brother.

1. What might this wrestling match symbolize?

2. How do we sometimes "wrestle" with God?

3. Why does the angel change Jacob's name? What "heart" change is represented by this name shift?

4. Why does the angel touch Jacob's hip, causing a limp?

5. How does Jacob respond to this seemingly "unfair" maneuver?

6. Overall, how does this wrestling encounter prepare Jacob for future events, beginning with his confrontation with Esau?

7. What are some of the "Esaus" in your life?

8. How has God changed you to overcome those "Esaus"?

Read Matthew 16:13-26. In this passage, Peter almost simultaneously establishes himself as the most right and the most wrong among the disciples.

1. How did Peter so quickly fall off track?

2. What should this tell us about our own vulnerability to sin?

3. Why was Peter so opposed to Christ's foretold suffering?

4. What former relationships in Peter's life may have influenced his thinking about the "Messiah"?

5. What were some of Peter's other struggles as he sought to enter in to intimacy with Christ? (*see* Mt 18:21–22; Mt 26:41–42; Mt 26:75; Jn 13:6–10; Jn 21:15–17)

6. How do these struggles compare to those we may have?

Look up the following scriptures: Romans 7:14–25; Romans 8:3–12; Galatians 5:13–26; 1 Peter 2:11.
1. What do these scriptures say about the struggle between flesh and spirit?

2. How do we overcome the "lusts of the flesh"?

3. How may these "fleshly" drives be derived from binding relationships to our past?

4. If we know that we are saved by faith, why does God still urge us to "come out and be separate"? (*see* 2 Cor 6:16–18)

5. What is the relationship between purity and intimacy? (*see* Mt 5:8)

Read Isaiah 54:5–8; Jeremiah 31:32–34; Revelation 21:2–7.

1. What are God's "wedding vows" to us, as expressed in these and other passages?

2. What does it mean to have the Lord as our husband?

3. How should that affect us practically in daily life?

Read Matthew 22:1-14.

1. In the parable of the wedding banquet, who does the King represent? The servants? The Son?

2. What do the garments represent? (*see* Col 3:5–14)

3. Why does the King become angry at the man who won't change his clothes?

4. Why do you think the man refused to change?

5. How does this compare to us?

Reflection

How much do you "know" your husband, Jesus Christ? What is holding you back from knowing him more?

What is the greatest struggle you face right now between the desires of your flesh and the needs of your spirit?

Make a list of unhealed hurts or needs that the Holy Spirit is prompting you to surrender for God's healing. Pray through each hurt or need separately, forgiving everyone involved, and asking God to restore this place in your heart.

List any habits or thinking patterns you have that oppose the will of God in your life. As you feel led, surrender each of these habits and thinking patterns to the Lord. Ask the Holy Spirit to reveal the "root" of these thoughts and behaviors to heal any underlying wounds that may be supporting those binding relationships.

Finally, identify any outstanding debt or unbroken contracts that may need to be given over to God's control. Once surrendered, God will begin, with your obedience, to show you how to get out of those unhealthy situations.

Don't forget to thank God as you witness the new sense of freedom and intimacy that results from the Holy Spirit's "spring cleaning" of your soul. Seek his strength and renewal daily through prayer and study of his Word. As you pray your way out of the binding relationships of your past life, it is very important that you simultaneously bind yourself more and more to the Lord. Remember, Jesus only brought up the Samaritan woman's past husbands in order to release her for a pure marriage to himself.

Establishing a Relationship of Worship

7

Scene 3 of the woman at the well story begins in John 4:19 when the woman acknowledges that Jesus must be some sort of prophet. Prior to this portion of their discourse, Jesus and the woman have already grappled with two crucial phases in the process of restoration: The invitation to accept living water (Scene 1, verses 4–15) and; the past (Scene 2, verses 16–18). Up to this point in the story, and even now, Jesus allows the woman to direct much of their conversation. Her own heart, like ours, introduces the issues that must be confronted for restoration.

It is significant that we understand the transition from Scenes 2 to 3. Jesus and the woman have been discussing her past husbands. As you will recall from the last lesson, their discussion served to release the woman from bondage to past relationships. In effect, Jesus was healing her by leading her to renounce and be released from these marriages in order that she might be consecrated (which means "to set apart as holy") for marriage to him. Her ultimate calling and heritage, just like ours and every other Christian's, is to be the Bride of Christ. However, that cannot fully occur until we are completely divorced from our previous "husbands." Thus, the Lord prompts the Samaritan woman to consider and be cleansed of the past.

The focus of their dialogue then seems to take a sudden shift in John 4:19–20, when the woman says, "Sir ... I can see that you are a prophet. Our fathers worshiped on this mountain, but you Jews claim that the place where we must worship is in Jerusalem." The most common interpretation I have heard of these verses suggests that the woman desired to "get Jesus off her back," and so she diverted attention away from her past by throwing out an irrelevant theological issue. I disagree with this interpretation.

I do not think the woman was avoiding uncomfortable conversation. I believe, for her, the matter of her past had been settled. As stated previously, we must remember two things about the Book of John as a whole: It is symbolic, and it is abbreviated. We need not think that simply because only a few lines are given to the issue of the five husbands that the matter was left unresolved. In fact, the woman's later testimony to the townspeople, "Come, see a man who told me everything I ever did (v. 29)," would suggest that there was more to their conversation than is actually recorded. Also, the positive impression of her testimony upon the people further supports the idea that, whatever was said, the woman experienced significant emotional healing through this encounter. Therefore, I propose a different interpretation of her question about where to worship.

During their discussion of the five husbands, the Lord worked with the Samaritan woman to restore her purity, to remove the stains of a painful past that had included multiple marriages to men (representing things of the world that disappoint and damage us). Through this healing process, the woman was prepared to enter into a new relationship with God as his Bride. Thus, her question regarding the place of worship follows naturally as a sincere request for information. Her heart, awakened to new desire and gratitude, cries out, "Where can I go to meet my husband?" When seen in this light, her question represents a very normal reaction of a reborn soul.

Jesus's response in verses 20-23 confirms this reading. He replies, "Believe me, woman, a time is coming when you will worship the Father neither on this mountain nor in Jerusalem. You Samaritans worship what you do not know, but we Jews worship what we do know, for salvation is from the Jews. Yet a time is coming and has now come when the true worshipers will worship the Father in spirit and truth, for they are the kind of worshipers the Father seeks." There are several significant points about this response.

First, Jesus uses the emphatic words, "Believe me" to draw attention to what follows. Throughout Scripture, when "signal" phrases like this (or the more common, "Truly, truly I say to you") are used, they serve to highlight what follows as an important truth of God's kingdom. Also, the word for "woman" used here is the Hebrew word *gune* which refers specifically to a wife. The Lord addresses the Samaritan woman, saying, "Listen closely, my wife," acknowledging both the importance of her question and his acceptance of her as his wife. This is the first time in their dialogue that He addresses her directly, and He uses an important relational term affirming the changes that are taking place in their relationship.

Jesus answers the woman's question in two parts. First, He addresses the place of worship. When she asks whether the proper place of worship was the Samaritan mountain (Mount Gerizim) or in Jerusalem (Mount Ebal), she acknowledges a longstanding disagreement between the Jews and the Samaritans. The history of these two mountains goes back to the days of Moses. The mountains exist about three kilometers apart. One is thickly forested and the other is completely bare. Together they provide a powerful, natural picture of the blessings and curses pronounced by Moses with regard to Israelite covenant law (Dt 11:29; 27:4–26). In later times, when the Israelites returned from captivity (having disobeyed the Law) they refused to allow the Samaritan, mixed-blood people, whose society had proliferated during their absence, to worship with them in the temple at Jerusalem (located on Mount Ebal). Thus, in defiance of this rejection, the Samaritans built a second temple on Mount Gerizim, the one the woman refers to in John 4:20.

Behind all of this history, which the woman holds up for Jesus to clarify, lies a very basic question we continue to ask to this day. In effect, she says, "I really want to experience God. So where must I go?" Today, in our age of revival, we might put it this way, "If I want to experience God, should I go to Kansas City or Toronto? First Baptist or Foursquare?" Even today, we tend to believe that God is somehow situated apart from us in these isolated places. Jesus's response applies as truly to us as it did to the woman at the well.

"Believe me, [my wife], a time is coming ... and has now come (v. 23) when you will worship the Father neither on this mountain nor in Jerusalem." In other words, the place of worship is irrelevant. The Amplified Bible reads, " you will not worship the Father (merely) on this mountain nor (merely) in Jerusalem." This version provides a more accurate understanding because the places themselves are not the problem. Rather, the problem lies in human hearts, which seek to define boundaries for God's Presence, methods for his worship, and means to explain, organize, and ultimately *control* everything God does. This timeless desire has existed within man since the earliest recorded times.

Genesis 11:1–9 relates the story of the tower of Babel. We can learn much from this experience of our ancestors. Despite punishing their pride and selfish ambitions, God had another reason for destroying the tower of Babel and confusing the languages of men. As long as the people focused their energy upon "building up" to experience God, they would never have found him. Their task was hopelessly misguided. They had completely missed the point. God would not be found in the religious forms of men's own design. Still today He is not found within the "long-baked bricks" (v. 3) of man's preconceived theological notions about who God is, where He can be found, or how He manifests himself in natural reality. As Jesus acknowledges in John 4:24, God is Spirit and must be worshiped in spirit and truth. He does not reside in temples (or towers) built by man, nor is He limited by the mind of man.

Thus, God confused the languages so that mankind would give up its mistaken pursuit and go deeper in its endeavor to understand one another and God. The bottom line of Jesus's response to the Samaritan woman, which applies all the more today in our age of revival, is this:

> *God is not limited to any place, method, or form of human worship, and we should be wary of placing too much stock in these external aids and manifestations. God resides in the willing hearts of those who love him and earnestly seek him.*

The Hebrew word for worship throughout this passage is *proskuneo* which means, among other things, "to kiss." If we desire to kiss the living God, to experience worship in its fullest sense, then we must do so on God's terms, not ours, according to his ways and the spiritual realm of his residence. Worship in its fullest sense represents a relational term expressing intimacy with a highly relational God. God wants to know us and for us to *know* him.

The second part of Jesus's response addresses this need for knowing. In verse 22, Jesus states, "You Samaritans worship what you do not *know*; we Jews worship what we do *know* for salvation is from the Jews." Jesus significantly uses the same root word for "know" in both cases—the word *eido* which denotes a "mechanical, passive, or casual vision." In this passage, Jesus pronounces a judgment against both the Samaritans and the Jews. On the one hand, He states that the Samaritans worship a God whom they have not known, even in a mechanical or casual sense. Despite all their efforts in building a second temple, they have not attained even the very lowest level of understanding. Then, Jesus continues, claiming the Jews worship a God they do know, or at least should know, because God has revealed his salvation through them. However, the word *eido* again used here suggests that Jesus credits their knowledge as mere surface-level understanding—a mechanical knowledge lacking the zeal of true intimacy. In both cases, the Lord identifies a lack of knowledge as the cause of human error in worship.

In Acts 17:22–25, the apostle Paul cites a similar criticism against the men of Athens. He states, "I see that in every way you are very religious. For as I walked around and looked carefully at your objects of worship, I even found an altar with this inscription: 'To an unknown God.' Now what you worship as something unknown, I am going to proclaim to you." Then, Paul goes on to introduce these men, members of the ruling Greek religious council (the Areopagus), to the knowledge of God through Jesus Christ. Like Jesus, Paul rebukes the people for their lack of knowledge and resulting error in worship—a criticism still well founded in our day. Many people today worship a God they do not know, and because they do not truly know him, they become subject to all sorts of false and oppressive doctrines that inhibit them from experiencing true intimacy with God.

Mike Bickle, in *Passion for Jesus*, states our current problem this way:

> We individual believers and the church as a whole possess so little of the knowledge of what God is truly like. Our ignorance of His diverse and glorious personality rots our religion. It leads to errors in our doctrines and contributes to the decay of *our confidence and passion in worship.* Our inadequate ideas about the personhood of God result in failure to develop deep affection for Jesus and to obey Him with fearless abandonment. Our faulty religious ideas of God damage our relationships with Him, deplete our prayer lives and drain the joy from our sacrificial service. (Creation House, 1994, p. 47)

Jesus's response to the woman at the well, like Paul's to the men of Athens, applies to the modern day church. It goes something like this: "You just don't get it. Worship has little to do with place or form and much to do with the attitudes of the human heart. Worship is not something you do *for* God, but something you do *with* God. It is an intimate exchange between an awesome Creator and his beloved child. Worship, from beginning to end, is uniquely experienced in the innermost chambers of holy intimacy, alone with God."

First Corinthians 13:12 states that in this life we only know in part. At our best, we still perceive as through a darkened glass. However, the verse ends by promising us that someday we shall know fully *even as we are fully known*. Many passages throughout the Bible describe how fully God knows us. One of my personal favorites is Psalms 139, especially verses 1–6. If I take the Corinthians promise literally, and I do, then I realize that someday I am going to know the Lord as fully as He knows me in Psalms 139:1–6. I will know when He sits and when He rises. I will discern his thoughts from afar (v. 2). I will be familiar with all his ways (v. 3). Even before He speaks a word, I will know it completely (v. 4). When I begin to think of the awesome implications of such intimacy with Almighty God, my spirit cries out with David, "Such knowledge is too wonderful for me, too lofty for me to attain! (v. 6)"

That is the kind of intimacy I desire to have with Jesus. Furthermore, I don't want to wait until Heaven to receive it, and I don't believe we have to. The Bible says that God has already given us the Holy Spirit as a deposit of our coming inheritance (Eph 1:13–14). First Corinthians 2:10–12 states that the Holy Spirit knows more about God than anyone else, and that his purpose is to help us understand "the things which are freely given to us of God." So if He is living in me while I am still on earth, I see no reason why I can't learn as much as my mortal frame can take about God right now.

Liberty Savard, in *Shattering Your Strongholds*, makes a point worth repeating about spiritual growth. She claims that God will never oppose us in our pursuit of him. Furthermore, she acknowledges that the devil cannot oppose us—he doesn't have the power to ultimately thwart our efforts to draw closer to God. The only one who can oppose our growth, according to Savard, is us (Bridge-Logos, 1997, p. 14).

So how do we oppose ourselves? Simply this: our lack of knowledge of Jesus Christ (Hos 4:6). We don't *know* whom we worship. Often we don't even know *how* to worship. Through the years we have so confused "worship" with "praise" that we spend a lot of time making noise and little time listening. We engage in much activity for God, yet we spend little time with God. We busy ourselves with *religion* all the while neglecting the greater priority—the stillness of *relationship*.

Psalms 46 offers an important premise with regard to worship. Verse 10 declares "Be still and know that I am God." The rest of this short psalm lists a variety of external manifestations of God's power, yet the worship principle at its heart remains simple: Be still. Many modern day believers have lost their understanding of what it means to be still and *know* God. In the pursuit of revival, many have been blinded by manifestations and have become overly concerned with defining what is and is not of God. From one extreme of rigidity to the other pole of disorder, we have become distracted by the *results* of worship, missing all the while the *purpose* of worship—to enter into an intimate embrace with God. We have traded one set of expectations for another—still baking bricks and piling up methods while God shakes his head and marvels at our confusion.

This is not to say that there is not an appropriate time and place for "noise" and celebration in our praise of God. However, we need to understand that the starting place for all worship is "being still" and knowing our God. Simply put, we need balance and truth to guard us from error. In his response to the woman at the well, Jesus did not say that worshiping the Father on either Mount Ebal or Mount Gerizim was wrong; He simply stated that those isolated occasions were not enough. God is Spirit, and He can be experienced anywhere, anytime, by those who seek to know him. Matthew 7:7 states, "Seek and ye shall find." When we earnestly seek the Lord, wherever we are and whatever humble method of praise and prayer we use, we will find him or, to state it more accurately, He will find *us*.

In this age of revival and world upheaval, we need more than ever to know God. To do so, we must regain our understanding of what it means to worship and what it means to be still. The inner silence of stilling ourselves should be the starting place for our every worship encounter. Furthermore, we must learn to hear his voice, and that can only happen when we quit talking and wait humbly for his response. Sometimes our greatest test of faith and our greatest act of worship occurs when we wait in silence before the King.

For reflection, I have asked you to meditate on Psalms 139 and 1 Corinthians 13:12. I have also asked you to spend at least one quiet time this week being still before the Lord. I encourage you to "tarry" with Jesus and reflect on what it means to worship (kiss) Almighty God (Mt 26:38–40). You might consider doing a study on the Greek word *meno,* which means to "tarry or abide," and purposefully seek to hear God's voice. All of these activities will support your pursuit of knowing him through worship.

Scripture Study

Begin by reviewing John 4:19–22. These verses comprise the first part of Scene 3 of Jesus's conversation with the woman at the well.

1. What is the central issue the woman raises? What does she *really* want to know?

2. In your own words, explain Jesus's two-part response.

3. What is significant about the way He addresses her? How would you react if He addressed you that way?

Read Genesis 11:1–9 (the story of Babel).

1. What can we learn from this story about worshiping God?

2. What did the people hope to accomplish by building a tower that reached to the heavens?

3. Are we still "building towers" and "names for ourselves" today? How?

4. Why exactly did God destroy the tower of Babel?

5. What do the "long baked bricks" stand for, and why did they offend God? (*see* Ex 20: 25–26)

6. Were the people drawing closer to God in their unified building effort?

7. What caution should that give us regarding humanitarian endeavors that are not God-ordained?

8. Why did God confuse their language?

Read Hosea 6:6; Matthew 9:13; and Matthew 12:7. This phrase occurs in both the Old and New Testaments and is quoted by Christ on two different occasions.

1. What does the Lord mean when He says He desires "mercy and not sacrifice"?

2. What is the difference between these two ways of worshiping?

3. According to God, which is more important and why? (*see also* 1 Sm 15:22–23)

4. How does this comply with what Jesus tells the Samaritan woman in John 4:21–23?

This leads to the second issue in Jesus's response.

1. What "judgment" does He state against the Samaritans in John 4:22? What does He say about the Jews?

2. What similar problem do both of these groups share?

3. What does this suggest as the starting place for worship?

Read Acts 17:22–25.
1. How is Paul's criticism of the men of Athens similar to Jesus's criticism of worship in his time?

2. Does this criticism apply to us today? How?

3. In your own words, what does it mean to "know God"?

4. How do we learn to "know" him? (*see* Ps 46)

5. What has helped you know him?

6. How would you like to know him more?

Reflection

Read Psalms 139:1-6 and 1 Corinthians 13:12. The Corinthians passage offers us a promise that someday we will know God as fully as He now knows us. Meditate on Psalms 139:1–6. These verses describe how thoroughly God knows you. Can you imagine what it will be like to know him that intimately? While the promise of 1 Corinthians 13:12 may not be fully realized until heaven, we should eagerly desire to realize as much of it as possible while still on earth. What are some practical steps you can take to know God better?

Reread Psalms 46. Try writing your own version of this psalm. Through what external events in your life have you learned to "be still and know" that God is who He says He is. Take a least one whole "quiet time" and "be still" before the Lord. Stillness represents an easily forgotten discipline within the Church. In the midst of busy lives and often crowded prayer times, we lose sight of our need to listen and just "be" with the Lord. How long has it been since you simply sat with the Lord (or went on a walk with him), allowing him to bring up topics for discussion rather than following your "prayer list"? Intercession is important, but so is time alone with God. Some days the greatest expression of our faith comes when we trust the Lord enough with our prayer requests to suspend them in favor of "quality time" with Jesus (*see* Mt 6:33).

Answer the following questions in your journal. In all honesty, do you know what it means to "be" with God? (*see* Mt 26:38—the word "tarry" comes from the Greek word *meno* which is also translated as "abide" in John 15) Despite all you may know *about* God, how much do you really *know* him? (*see* Mt 7:21–23)

Worship in Spirit and Truth

8

Without a doubt, the most frequently cited passage from the woman at the well story involves the phrase "worship in spirit and truth." This passage occurs in the second half of Scene 3 (Jn 4:19–26) and represents one of Jesus's most direct commentaries regarding how humans are to relate to God. The concept of worship in spirit and truth has received considerable attention throughout church ages, and not a few Christian publications have sought to expound its meaning. In this chapter, we will investigate that concept in context and see how it relates to the greater story of restoration, within which it has been so skillfully woven.

In Lesson 7, we studied the transition from the five husbands (Scene 2) to the discussion of worship (Scene 3). We investigated how this transition flowed naturally when understood in context. Once the woman had been released from the husbands of her past (representing binding relationships), she was prepared to enter a new relationship with Jesus Christ as her seventh husband—the number of completeness. Thus, she inquires where to go and, by implication, what to do to experience God.

Jesus responds in two parts. First, He explains that the place of worship is irrelevant, as are other external forms and means of human worship. God is Spirit and therefore He exists outside whatever devices mankind creates to codify worship into a set of rules and methods. This is not to say that certain places, songs, teachings, and so forth are bad; but they must be kept in perspective. Furthermore, we should not wait for perfect circumstances to worship. Rather, worship involves an intimate exchange of the heart. God can and will be known by the willing hearts who seek him.

Secondly, Jesus points out a lack of knowledge as the major hindrance to worship among both the Samaritans and Jews. Thus, He establishes that knowing God represents the first and foremost "act" of worship. From Psalms 46, we learned that "being still" is one way to know God—a way that many people today have forgotten or failed ever to learn.

Thus, we arrive at the second half of this discourse on worship. In verses 23–24, Jesus states, "But the hour cometh, and now is when the true worshipers shall worship the Father in spirit and in truth:

for the Father seeketh such to worship him. God is a Spirit: and they that worship him must worship him in spirit and in truth" (KJV). These two verses are perhaps the most significant and most often cited passages of the story of the woman at the well. Many books and articles have been written in an attempt to unlock the full meaning of these verses, and I certainly do not profess to present the definitive meaning here. I do wish, however, to offer one explanation drawn from the context within which the phrase is given.

As we have seen, these verses flow out of a larger discussion of worship. More importantly, these verses are situated in the middle of a story of restoration, and thus they represent a central pillar of that truth. Taken as a whole, the story of the woman at the well amounts to a beautiful picture of restoration, expressing God's heart to re-build a broken people, one life at a time. When seen in that context, Jesus and the Samaritan woman's discussion of worship becomes an outflow of the restoration and healing that Jesus is bringing about in her life. In other words, He heals her of her past and leads her to a place where she may be rightly restored in relationship with him as his Bride. She poses a question, "How do I worship God?" or "How should I relate to you?" and He answers. First, He corrects her mistaken ideas about worship, and then He goes on to explain exactly how one is to worship God. He provides clear guidelines for establishing a worship relationship with the Father.

You may remember from the last chapter that worship in Hebrew means, "to kiss." To worship God means to kiss the living God—a very intimate picture. According to the *American Heritage Dictionary*, the word worship means: "(1) ardent, humble devotion; and (2) to love or pursue devotedly." I particularly like the second definition. To understand worship, we need to get out of thinking that it is a single act, something equal to praise. We often hear the terms "praise" and "worship" used together and many of us have come to think these terms are interchangeable, both referring to singing, shouting, making music, clapping, or dancing. However, worship amounts to something different from praise. Praise is typically an outward expression while worship, on the other hand, suggests an inward response. Unlike praise, which may be loud and boisterous at times, worship generally remains more intimate and often quiet. Worship involves a dedicated pursuit: a focused passion sustained long term rather than isolated experiences of celebration.

In John 4:23–24, Jesus explains that God must be worshiped in spirit and truth. In this phrase, He establishes two important boundaries to guide our walk with God. It is as though the Lord says, "Okay, you want to know God. Here's how you do it. God is Spirit, so to fully understand him you must come to understand him both in the spiritual realm and in his truth.

These two boundaries are like the guardrails around a racetrack. The inner rail represents worship in spirit. This refers to knowing God through intimate, spiritual experiences. Such experiences often occur during times of intense adoration, prayer, or meditation. They take place when we are willing to go beyond what we see and know through our natural eyes and allow the Holy Spirit to lead us into the supernatural throne room of God. To worship in spirit means we accept God as Spirit and desire to encounter him as He is in the spiritual realm. Often, spiritual worship experiences occur through dreams, visions, and other manifestations of God's Presence and power, which to many of us have been largely unknown. These experiences may initially catch us off guard or even offend our natural minds. They may seem strange because they are uncomfortable to our natural ways of thinking. They challenge our control. They defy our explanation. Ultimately, they confront us with a God who is much bigger, vaster, more holy, more powerful, and more loving than we ever imagined. Such experiences transform us and lead us in ever increasing intimacy with the Father. They occur on the inner track.

Worship in truth represents the outer guardrail of the racetrack. This boundary is more familiar to most of us. It involves the full truth of God's Word. In John 14:6, Jesus said, "I am the Way and the Truth and the Life. No one comes to the Father except through me." We know that the central purpose of the Word of God is to proclaim the good news of Jesus Christ. Everything in the Bible until Christ points to his birth and everything after that points back to his life, death, and resurrection. Thus, worship in truth means a devoted pursuit of the knowledge of God through his Word. The Word represents for us an outer boundary to protect us and to separate us from the world (which lies outside the racetrack).

Now, a couple of interesting points about auto racing. First, those on the inner track travel the fastest, often reaching speeds of 150–200 miles per hour. Because race cars are not equipped with power steering, it is very difficult to make the turns, especially on the inner track where the turns are sharpest and approached at such high speeds. On the inner track, there are great possibilities for error since each maneuver requires intense concentration and strength. This is much like traveling the inner track of worship in spirit. I liken it to a dance with fast, intricate steps. As we learn to dance this dance of intimacy with God in a spiritual realm to which most of us are unaccustomed, we have a great potential for making mistakes.

That is why we need the outer guardrail of truth. In auto racing, the outer guardrail serves to keep those drivers who have lost control from being thrown off track, which would destroy the car and potentially injure innocent onlookers. Again, this alludes to a powerful spiritual parallel. As we seek to know God more in the spiritual realm (which is the greater need of most believers and churches), we must always maintain a close adherence to God's truth. That way, even if we make mistakes when interpreting visions or exercising fledgling gifts, we will not give place for Satan to destroy us or for us to inadvertently wound the spectators of our lives.

Another point about auto racing: Racing fans attend races primarily for two reasons. First, they want to see how different cars perform under pressure. And second, they come to see the wrecks. This is very similar to the way the world watches Christians. They want to see how we perform under pressure: Do we live what we preach? Also, they want to see our wrecks. Imagine a diagram of a racetrack. On either side of the track are grandstands. Label one grandstand "love of the natural," and the other "fear of man," both referring to the world that daily surrounds us.

If we are to be serious "racers," intent on pursuing worship in spirit and truth, we have no time to be worried about spectators. Just like in auto racing, the minute we look away from the wheel and the track in front of us, several things may happen. For one thing, we may begin to slow down. If that happens, our car will naturally drift upwards (because the track is slanted) and we will begin to lose our place on the inner track of spiritual worship. We will lose our focus.

If we continue losing focus and control (which naturally follows), we may end up crashing. If we have been faithful to continue our pursuit of worship in truth, the outer guardrail will protect us from zooming out into the world or injuring others. As we drift upward and brush against this rail, the car will be turned (by the slanted roadway and the momentum of our continued relationship with God) and we will be sent back towards the middle of the track. Thus, working together, the guardrails of spirit and truth will keep us on track despite whatever drifting (or even crashing) we may do in between.

There are many excellent Scriptures on truth. I encourage you someday to do a word study on "truth" to better understand the role of God's Word in our daily walk with him. For additional study, I selected only a few Scriptures to look up, all from the Psalms: 40:11; 51:6; 91:4; 145:18; 146:5–6. These Scriptures explain how God's truth serves to protect us in our "inward parts" (Ps 51:6). The Word of God is our shield and our sword (Eph 6), a vital part of the armor of God. We cannot underestimate the importance of maintaining a close adherence to God's Word. In *The Final Quest*, Rick Joyner compares God's Word to a sword that grows larger with each battle serving to anchor us on the slippery ledges of the highest levels of spiritual warfare (Whitaker House, 1996, p. 41). As we begin to experience the glorious intimacy of worship in spirit, we must remember not to abandon an equal pursuit of God's truth. Both are necessary for growth and maturity in our relationship with Jesus Christ.

To understand this balance better, let's look at a few examples of worshipers in Scripture. First, we will look at Mary of Bethany. In Luke 10:38–42, we read the story of Mary and Martha. Jesus comes to their home where He reclines and shares an intimate conversation with some of his closest disciples. At his feet Mary sits, soaking in his every word. Meanwhile, Martha works feverishly in the kitchen to provide a plentiful meal for the disciples. Finally, she's had enough and complains to Jesus, asking him to tell Mary to come and help her. Jesus replies, "Martha, Martha, you are worried and upset about many things, but only one thing is needed. Mary has chosen what is better, and it will not be taken away from her" (v. 41–42).

Martha was not wrong in preparing food for the disciples. Jesus himself had said, "And if anyone gives even a cup of cold water to one of these little ones ... he will certainly not lose his reward" (Mt 10:42). Here Martha was serving a pot roast to many in Jesus's name—thus, the act itself was not wrong. In fact, one could say she was worshiping the Lord in the truth of his own instructions. She loved him and desired to exercise her gift for hospitality. However, while she raced furiously around the outer track, something much more meaningful was taking place in her very own living room.

Mary, Martha's sister, realized the greater opportunity. She was worshiping in spirit and knew the Lord would not be with them much longer. Absorbed by her love for him, Mary desired the intimacy of his Presence more than anything else. She chose to go beyond the needs and perceptions of the natural, including the social taboos of a woman sitting at the feet of a Jewish rabbi, and experience the inner track of spiritual intimacy. Unlike Martha, Mary remained focused. She held on. Furthermore, she was not displaced by the misunderstanding of those outside that intimate circle. She sought the approval of only One, and in so doing she "kissed" the living God.

In Matthew 26:6–16, we read of another time when Mary "kissed" Jesus. This time they were in the home of Simon the Leper. The Scripture says that as Jesus reclined at the table, a woman came with an alabaster jar of expensive perfume, poured the perfume on Jesus's feet, and wiped them with her hair. The Book of John tells us that this woman was Mary, Martha's sister. When Mary blessed Jesus in this way, the disciples sharply rebuked her. However, Jesus came to her defense saying, "Leave her alone. She has done a beautiful thing to me ... I tell you that wherever this gospel is preached throughout the world, what she has done will also be told, in memory of her" (v. 10,13). Jesus acknowledged Mary's act of worship as a "beautiful thing."

There are several interesting aspects of this story. First, Mary's act was both symbolic and prophetic. The alabaster jar and expensive perfume provide a powerful picture of what it is we offer the Lord through our worship. Some say that this jar and its costly contents represented Mary's dowry, the means by which she could have someday secured a husband. Thus, pouring this perfume on Jesus's feet demonstrates both Mary's willingness to surrender all of her life to the Lord and her recognition in a spiritual sense that Jesus was her only true husband. The alabaster jar can also represent our lives, our hearts, and our willingness to give all that we have to honor Jesus. The perfume represents our worship and praise, which spill out of a surrendered life, a broken and contrite spirit (Ps 51:17), to fill the air with a fragrant aroma of the knowledge of Jesus Christ (2 Cor 2:14–15). Like the rock at Horeb, the alabaster jar symbolizes the power of God to bring forth rivers of living water in even the most desolate circumstances and hearts once surrendered to him (Ex 17:6).

Mary's act was also prophetic. Mary understood, perhaps more vividly than any of the other disciples at the time, that Jesus was about to die. She was interpreting his words on a much deeper level than the others as evident by the appropriateness of her actions. Jesus said, "She has done this to prepare me for burial" (Mt 26:12). Mary's act, much like those of the Old Testament prophets, signified or "prophesied" the coming will of God. Like Samuel anointing David to be king, Mary anointed the Lord for the death by which He would save the world.

When we enter into the intimacy of true worship, we will begin to understand the Lord's heart in new ways. We will begin to fellowship with him on deeper levels in the sweet inner chambers of God's heart. In the midst of a rather hostile crowd, Mary experienced an intimate moment with the Lord through worship. She was able to do so because she was willing to risk embarrassment and misunderstanding. The disciples didn't understand and they rebuked her harshly. However, I do not believe their contention arose from wasted expense as much as it did their envy of her intimate experience.

This story of the anointing at Bethany occurs in all four gospels, an initial fulfillment of Christ's promise that "wherever this gospel is preached throughout the world, this story will be told in memory of her." In three of the four gospels, this story is immediately followed by Judas's arrangement with the elders of Israel to betray Jesus. The sequence of these two accounts is no coincidence. Satan gets very nervous when the people of God discover the pathway to true worship. The devil, who once led worship in heaven (Is 42:11–15), knows the power of such intimacy for transforming lives and advancing the kingdom of God. Mary's act of worship initiated a whole new level of abandonment in love to Jesus Christ. As a result, all "hell" broke loose. The prince of darkness grew anxious and prompted many of the disciples, most significantly Judas, to take offense at this extremely intimate, "beautiful" act of worship. Judas left that place filled with religious indignation, which Satan used to deceive him into betraying the Son of God (Mt 26:14–16). We must avoid judging others' worship lest we fall prey to the same trap.

One final note on Mary's worship. When the disciples rebuked her, she did not give place to their offense. She did not defend herself, but allowed the Lord to take up her rebuttal. We can learn from her in this regard. There will be times when others do not understand our ways of worshiping God. And while we should try to be sensitive to the "little ones" in the Lord and do all we can to keep them from stumbling (for in this way we worship in accordance with the truth of Mt 18:6,14), we must be discerning and willing to worship as the Holy Spirit directs us, even if that means risking some measure of personal embarrassment or misunderstanding. Furthermore, if and when we are misunderstood by those who are caught up in the natural discomforts of supernatural worship, we should not take it upon ourselves to right the situation but allow the Lord to do so according to his own time and fashion. As Jesus told the people in Matthew 11:19, "wisdom is proved right by her actions."

There is one more example of worship to examine in Luke 2:1–14. It is the story of Jesus's birth. When I first asked the Lord to direct me to examples of worship in Scripture, this story immediately came to mind. It is the story of another Mary who knew what it meant to go beyond the natural in worship.

When Mary first learned that she was pregnant with the Child of God, I am sure she made plans for his arrival. Once she got past Joseph's initial rejection and learned to cope with the rejection of the townspeople, she must have begun to daydream about what it would be like to raise the Son of God. In all her plans, however, I doubt Bethlehem ever came up.

I would imagine, if she had had a choice, she would not have journeyed to Bethlehem. Perhaps she was required to go, or perhaps there was simply no one behind to help her if she had gone into labor. It may be that the fear of going into labor alone outweighed the difficulty and risk of traveling in her ninth month. Whatever propelled her to go, I can only imagine her fear when she felt those first few contractions. She must have thought, "Oh no ... what are we going to do now?" As inn after inn turned them away, I am sure her fears magnified even more. Here she was preparing to have her firstborn with no place to lie down, no midwife, no family as-sistance, no cradle—nothing. I wonder if somewhere in the midst of that pain and fear she felt like crying out, "Where are you, God? What's going on?"

Despite her fears and the inadequacy of their circumstances, the baby came. If Mary had had a choice, I wonder if she would have tried to stop the labor. Instead, she gave birth in a cow stall and laid the newborn child in a feedbox. I am sure that was not what she had planned. With Joseph being a carpenter, I feel certain they had a beautifully carved cradle waiting back home for them along with carefully knit baby clothes and all other necessary supplies.

The marvel of this story is that Mary "labored through the natural" to encounter the Living God. I can only dream what it must have been like to hold God in her arms. This was the first time since the Fall of man that God had openly revealed himself to commoners. In his Presence, there must have been overwhelming peace, joy, and love—all the spiritual attributes of God clothed in human flesh. When Mary placed her lips against Jesus's newborn cheeks, she kissed the Living God. As previously stated, the word for worship in Hebrew means "to kiss." Through her humble obedience, Mary worshiped.

The main thing we learn from Mary in this story concerns the importance of "laboring through the natural." Often, the circumstances of worship are not what we would like or expect them to be. We may not like the songs that day. We may not "feel" up to the task. However, if we will be faithful to look beyond our natural discomforts and submit to the will of God, we will be delivered and we will kiss God in ways we never dreamed possible. For each of us, there is a season of labor that may be uncomfortable, even downright painful. However, if we press on through those circumstances, God will birth his eternal purposes in our lives and lead us into greater intimacy with him than we have ever known.

For reflection, I have asked you to consider some questions to determine where you need to grow in your worship relationship with the Lord. Are you balanced in your relationship with Christ, or do you lean too much toward either spirit or truth? What practical steps could you take to establish a better balance? Where do you most need to grow?

Scripture Study

In this chapter, we focused in on the phrase "worship in spirit and truth." This is one of the most significant passages in all of Scripture in terms of defining how we are to worship God. To understand this passage, we must first view it in context.

1. How do verses 23–24 of John fit in with the rest of Scene 3?

2. How do they fit within the whole story of the woman at the well?

3. What do they suggest about the goal of restoration?

Before we look at scriptural examples of worship, consider the following questions:

1. What does it mean to worship in spirit? In truth?

2. What have you been taught in the past about personal worship?

3. What have you learned so far from John 4 that has enhanced or changed those views?

Read the following passages on truth from the Psalms: Ps 40:11; 51:6; 91:4; 145:18; 146:5–6.

1. What do these passages suggest about God's truth?

2. What is the function of truth in a believer's life?

(Note: We will study "worship in spirit" more in Lesson 9 when we investigate spiritual gifts.)

Now let's shift gears and apply what we've learned about worship to a few examples in Scripture. **Read Luke 10:38–42.**
1. What challenges you from this passage about worship?

2. In what ways was Martha wrong?

3. Have you ever made similar mistakes?

Now read Matthew 26:6–16.
1. What does this story show us about worship?

2. How does "hell" respond to Mary's act?

3. What is the difference in Martha's "worship" as compared to Mary's?

4. How can these ways of worshiping be balanced, both in our personal lives and in the church?

Finally, let's look at one more example. **Read Luke 2:1–14.**

1. List all the acts of worship that are suggested in this passage.

2. How does Mary "kiss" God through her travail?

3. What is the response of "heaven" ?

4. What does this teach us about engaging the supernatural (or spiritual) in worship?

Reflection

In your journal, respond to the following questions:

1. Where are you on the "racetrack" of worship?

2. Is your personal worship time somewhat lopsided, favoring either worship in spirit or worship in truth?

3. What steps could you take to correct this imbalance?

4. Are you currently having regular, personal worship time with God? If not, why?

5. What, if anything, have you been taught in the past about how to have a "quiet time" with God?

6. What would you like to know more about to enhance your "quiet times"?

7. Who are you most comfortable relating to: God the Father, God the Son, or God the Holy Spirit? What part of God are you least comfortable relating to? Why?

8. In your own words, define what it means to "worship in spirit"?

The Role of Spiritual Gifts in Worship

9

One of the most important ways we learn to worship God in spirit occurs through the discovery and release of spiritual gifts. Over the years, the emphasis on spiritual gifts has ebbed in and flowed out of church life in a somewhat trendy fashion. Many people enjoy taking spiritual gifts tests, which are designed similarly to personality and I.Q. tests, to discover their particular bent for church service. Unfortunately, it seems to me that very few—and I mean *very few*—ever do much with what they learn about themselves. Rather, we tend to treat spiritual gifts with the same nonchalance as other matters of spiritual maturity—acting as if the whole Christian growth process and our willingness to fulfill our part of the Body remains optional.

I doubt that we really need these spiritual gifts tests. After all, the early church didn't have them, and neither did the woman at the well. Not to say these tests aren't helpful, but I do think they may create a self-consciousness about giftings that inhibits rather than promotes their release in our lives. The fault is not in the test, but in our response to its conclusions. John 4 gives no indication that the Samaritan woman consulted anyone, including Jesus, about what her gifts were, and yet she launched an evangelism campaign that transformed her entire town. She wasn't at all self-conscious about doing this, either. She sought no approval; she needed no one's permission and no test slip confirmation that evangelism really was her gift.

Instead, the Samaritan woman simply gave what she herself had recently received. She testified to what she knew. She shared what it was like to be known. Whatever it was she said and did, the townspeople were deeply affected. Without even realizing it, the Samaritan woman exercised a fledgling spiritual gift for evangelism with powerful results (Jn 4:39–42).

In the past two lessons, we have been studying what it means to worship God in a relational, intimate sense. Corporately, we are all called to be his worshipers. The Bible says we were created to glorify God (Is 43:6–7; Col 1:16). Within that corporate calling, however, each of us has been given unique gifts and abilities to "kiss" God, to bring him pleasure, and to further the desires of his heart that involve building up the Church and "harvesting" lost souls (Jn 4:34–35).

Thus, part of learning to worship in spirit necessarily involves coming to understand the role of spiritual gifts in worship—both as an individual and collectively as the Body of Christ.

First Corinthians 12–14 contains some of the most significant teaching in the Bible regarding spiritual gifts. The context of this teaching bears much significance. Before launching into a discussion of spiritual gifts, Paul spends the first eleven chapters of this epistle straightening out divisions and petty squabbles of Corinthian church members. Over and over Paul reminds them that they are one body and should seek to serve one another. Then he begins to clarify how such service should proceed through spiritual gifts.

One of the most important directives Paul gives about spiritual gifts occurs in 1 Corinthians 12:7: "Now to each one the manifestation of the Spirit is given for the *common good.*" When studying spiritual gifts, we must always remember God's purpose for giving them. Spiritual gifts are individual distributions of God's grace for the common good of the Church. Whatever gifts we may possess are wholly of God for his people. We are merely the vessels that contain them.

I once attended a gathering of more than 9,000 Christian women from all over the world. Many of the ladies were adorned in their native dress during the meetings. The display of so many different cultures was truly remarkable. As I waited for one of the morning sessions to begin, I marveled at just how many billions and billions of people God had created since the beginning of time. Inevitably the question rose in my mind, "Why, God? Why so many different people?"

In response, the Holy Spirit led to me to think of a good friend named Janice. He said:

> If you listed all of Janice's attributes—a complete list of the unique qualities that make up her character, you could compile a list of 100 or more traits. All the people who have ever been or will be created, every living human, represents a distinct attribute of God. Together, you represent the fullness of My character.

The unique combination of spiritual gifts and personality that God has ordained within each of us allows us the awesome privilege of representing him as no other human being can. Our individuality runs far deeper than most of us realize. Because we each possess a single attribute of God unlike any other, we have a precious ability to interrelate with and bless him, which no one else can experience. To think of how many unique combinations and distinct traits we collectively possess only enhances our appreciation of how vast, ingenious, and truly amazing our God is.

As we begin to understand the intimacy of true worship, and the balance of spirit and truth that supports that relationship, we will be inevitably awakened to desire a deeper knowledge of God through spiritual gifts. Moreover, we will yearn to know the Holy Spirit who ignites and sustains these gifts. Speaking of the Holy Spirit, 1 Corinthians 2:10–12 states: "The Spirit searches all things, even the deep things of God. For who among men knows the thoughts of a man except the man's spirit within him? In the same way, no one knows the thoughts of God except the Spirit of God. We have not received the spirit of the world but the Spirit who is from God, that we may understand what God has freely given us."

God has chosen the Holy Spirit to empower us from within, to give us understanding, and to remind us of all the teachings of Christ (Jn 14:26). Without the Spirit, we cannot hope to live a victorious Christian life. He is our power from on high (Lk 24:49). No matter how much we know about God, about Jesus, or about our spiritual inheritance, the Spirit alone translates that understanding into power and renewed life (Jn 6:63; 2 Cor 3:6). He is called the *paraclete* which means "one who comes alongside," and that is his function (Jn 16:7). The Holy Spirit comes alongside believers and enables them to move from head knowledge to heartfelt relationship with Jesus Christ (Jn 16:7–11).

There are two distinct byproducts of the Spirit's Presence in a believer's life. One evidence involves the "fruit" of the Spirit as described in Galations 5:22: "The fruit of the Spirit is love, joy, peace, patience, kindness, goodness, gentleness, faithfulness, and self-control." These attributes represent Christ's character, godly seedlings which the Spirit "transplants" into the hearts and lives of maturing believers. Secondly, the Spirit's Presence also produces spiritual gifts. First Corinthians 12:8–10 lists nine such gifts (just as there are nine "fruits") including: wisdom, knowledge, faith, healing, miracles, prophecy, discerning of spirits, speaking in tongues, and interpretation of tongues. Romans 12:6–8 also mentions gifts of service, teaching, encouragement, giving, administration, and mercy. Like "fruit," each of these gifts provides evidence of the Holy Spirit working in and through a believer's life.

In the past, there has been much disagreement regarding the procedures through which one may receive the Holy Spirit. In fact, issues surrounding the Holy Spirit (most notably speaking in tongues) have caused a grievous amount of discord among the brethren—very similar to the divisions Paul addresses in the first eleven chapters of Corinthians before he addresses the topic of spiritual gifts. God never intended for the Holy Spirit to be a thorn in the Church's side causing countless factions and controversies. However, because He is so mysterious to us—like the wind, unseen and uncontrollable (Jn 3:8)—our human minds desperately struggle to define his "boundaries."

The Bible gives many different accounts of ways in which people received the Holy Spirit. Sometimes elders laid hands on them, sometimes they didn't (Acts 8:17; 19:6; 10:44). Sometimes the recipients spoke in tongues, other times tongues are not mentioned (Acts 10:44–46; 8:14–17). Some people received visions, others received power, still others received words of insight beyond human ability (Acts 8:29; 10:19–21). The accounts are so varied, and so beautifully personalized, that it would be impossible to codify them all into one way or means by which the Spirit is received.

The bottom line is this: God is a God of incredible individuality. He meets each of us where we are and leads us in whatever way we need to be led. Some people need loud, external evidence of the Spirit's indwelling; others need only the quiet assurance of a new peace or ability to interpret God's Word. Initial manifestations are not nearly as important as the long-term change that follows this release, what many call "the baptism of the Holy Spirit."

Does someone have to lay hands on you for you to receive the Holy Spirit? Do you have to speak in tongues? In my opinion, no. At least not initially. As a believer, you can simply ask for the Holy Spirit in Jesus's name, and the Father will send him to you (Mt 7:7–11). Now there may come a time when you will desire to experience the laying on of hands or the power of a prayer language in order to be more fully *released* in the Spirit, but initially you simply need to ask. The Holy Spirit, like salvation, is a gift that cannot be earned through any means of performance or method (Jn 20:21–22; Rev 22:17).

How do you know when you have received the Holy Spirit? Simple: by the evidence of his Presence which we discussed previously. Wherever the Spirit resides, He produces the fruit of Christlike character. Moreover, He inspires righteousness and service among the Body and toward the Lost. He releases his gifts and empowers believers to overcome sin and perform deeds far beyond their fleshly abilities (Acts 3:4–7; 4:8–13). He encourages unity and selflessness (Eph 4:3–7). He grants freedom to those who are oppressed (Is 61). He heals the brokenhearted. He gives joy and peace beyond circumstantial merit (Rom 14:17). He provides wisdom, light, and love in increasing measure. And He always exalts Jesus Christ (Jn 14:26).

By his fruit we recognize the Spirit in individual lives; by his gifts we address him corporately. Though each of the gifts operate through individuals, the Bible clearly states they are given with corporate goals in mind. In other words, as we seek to understand those gifts which the Lord has placed within our own lives, we must always keep an eye out to what He is doing in our local congregation. There is a great danger in separating teaching on spiritual gifts from the context of the local church. The local church represents the "common denominator" for individual members of Christ's body. At any given time, God will raise up those who have gifts that are needed to meet the local church's needs. This is a hard concept for Americans today, many of whom have bought into the idea that we each live and die to ourselves and for ourselves, accountable for no one but ourselves. At least as far as spiritual gifts are concerned, the Bible takes a different perspective.

We are gifted to serve, not just so that we can feel good about ourselves. Yes, each of us is special to God as an individual, but even more so because we have an irrevocable part to play in the great drama of his Bride. As Mike Bickle so eloquently states in *Passion for Jesus*, we don't merely have an inheritance in God; He has an inheritance in us. As much as He desires to grow us up and bless us, He hopes that we will someday join his passionate pursuit of the Lost (Creation House, Ch. 8, p. 3).

That's the beauty of the woman at the well. When she discovers who Jesus really is, she doesn't just take it all in and sit there. Instead, she leaves her water jar and runs back to the town, to the very people who despised and mistreated her, and begins to tell them about Jesus. Without even taking a "gifts" test, she launches headlong into full scale evangelism. She didn't even go to Bible school first! She wasn't ordained! No one laid hands on her! She didn't take a month to pray about it! She just responded out of the pure and overwhelming passion of newly ignited love for Jesus. And, generally speaking, that is all it takes. We are the ones who make it so complicated.

As we learned in Lesson 7, worship is not limited or driven by anything in the natural. Rather, worship begins as an intimate, spiritual exchange between God and his child. At its best, worship means kissing God. It begins when we quiet ourselves long enough to listen to the Spirit's still, small voice. Then, as we move out from that initial place into the realm of truth and service, our hearts never leave the sanctuary of God's holy, loving embrace.

In 1 Corinthians 12–14, Paul establishes three practical points about spiritual gifts. First, he emphasizes their unity. In Chapter 12, verses 4–6, Paul writes: "There are different kinds of gifts, but the same Spirit. There are different kinds of service, but the same Lord. There are different kinds of working, *but the same God works all of them in all men.*" It is very important to realize that no one gift is any greater than another. As Chuck Smith states in *Living Water*, "What are the best gifts? The best gifts are those which can best accomplish the task at hand" (Harvest House, 1996, p. 94). A long time ago, the Lord taught me that only humans love comparatives and superlatives, or "ranking" words. God does not rank things or people the way we do. He is much more selective when He establishes the "good, better, and bests" of life. God has appointed all spiritual gifts because every one is needed to ensure a healthy Church.

Secondly, Paul acknowledges to the Corinthians in Chapter 12:28–30 that spiritual gifts are given in conjunction with whatever office one is serving within the local congregation. Many people often wonder why they do not know what their spiritual gifts are. Perhaps it is because they are not currently serving in a local gathering of believers. In verses 28–30, Paul establishes a direct link between one's gifts and one's office, an idea that Chuck Smith elaborates in Chapter 7 of *Living Water*. I have heard it suggested that each of us has only one or two gifts with absolutely no ability to move in the others. As Smith explains, gifts often come in groups as necessary for whatever office God has called an individual to hold. For example, someone called to teach in the local body may be gifted with wisdom, knowledge, and prophecy. Or someone called to work in a Christian pregnancy center may be gifted with mercy, wisdom, and helps. In the course of time, gifts may change according to church needs, the Lord's will, and our own growth in spiritual maturity (Eccl 3:1; 8:5–6).

Incidentally, I do not believe that Paul intended for his listing of spiritual gifts to be understood as comprehensive (Rom 12; 1 Cor 9, 12). After all, Paul knew very well what it felt like to think one knows everything about God and to be proven wrong. A man who's been knocked off his horse learns to ride more cautiously. (Acts 9:3–5). I doubt that this same man would turn around a few years later and claim full knowledge of the Holy Spirit's operation. Rather, I believe Paul's listing of spiritual gifts is exemplary, merely a sketch of what may be found in the total Person of the Holy Spirit. Obviously, there can be as many different types of gifts as there are aspects of God's character. The gifts demonstrate God's abilities to interact with and minister to his people. We are foolish to box God in by attempting to force all his children into such a small model. I think Paul would have laughed at that suggestion. Furthermore, he would likely reprimand us as he did the Corinthians for being so limited in our thinking (1 Cor 14:20).

The Holy Spirit empowers us to move in all the gifts we see demonstrated in Jesus Christ. In our thinking about spiritual gifts, we must resist imagining that we possess only certain abilities and are inevitably cut off from others. Thus, when a need arises in a certain area of ministry, we shrink back from the opportunity because it seems to fall outside what we perceive our anointing to be. Certainly, it is beneficial to know oneself in the Lord and to purposefully seek out one's role in the local fellowship of believers. However, Philippians 4:13 says we can do "all things through Christ who gives [us] strength." The anointing we carry is the Spirit of Jesus Christ, and He equips us "to do any good work" as we yield ourselves to him by faith (2 Tm 2:21). We will likely move more freely and effectively in certain venues of ministry more than others, but Colossians 4:5 says we are to "make the most of every opportunity" presented to us. Our self-knowledge must remain balanced by God's omnipotence working through us.

Once I sought the Lord for an explanation concerning how we move in spiritual gifts. In response, He showed me a landscape. In this horizon there were distinct high peaks and low-lying valleys. The Holy Spirit explained:

> *Each person's personality is like this horizon. The valleys represent areas in which that person is particularly "gifted" to be sensitive to God. As the water of the Holy Spirit is released and begins to flow in that person's life, these areas will fill up first. However, as that person continues to mature, the water level will rise until even the peaks are covered by My anointing and grace.*

Each of us may be particularly sensitive to God in certain ways. These represent our primary giftings, our natural bents and passions, which may or may not change throughout the course of our lives. However, when we receive the Holy Spirit, we receive all of him. He is wholly present with us throughout our lives. Thus, it is not a question of whether we do or do not have a particular gift, but whether God has released that gift in us for the season or office in which we are currently serving.

The third point Paul makes about spiritual gifts occurs in Chapter 13. This is perhaps the most important point of all—the role of love in spiritual gifts. In the final verse of Chapter 12, after listing many different gifts, Paul concludes: "Eagerly desire the greater gifts. And now I will show you the most excellent way" (v. 31). Then he begins what is commonly called "the love chapter," which describes the inner and outer expressions of holy love. Chapter 13 ends with the following words: "And now these three remain: faith, hope and love. But the greatest of these is love."

Love is the ultimate expression of worship. More than any fruit or gift, love encompasses the mission of the Holy Spirit. Greater still, love embodies the nature of God and the Person of Jesus Christ. Love fulfills all law and represents the perfect balance of spirit and truth in worship (Rom 13:10). It involves both action and emotion. It is thoughtful, forbearing, hopeful, gentle, and patient in every circumstance (1 Cor 13:4). Love is never hasty or rude (1 Cor 13:5). It never forsakes its object or yields to the pressures of performance. Perfect love casts out all fear and demolishes the religious strongholds that choke our passion for God (1 Jn 4:18). Love *is* worship. "It always protects, always trusts, always hopes, always perseveres. Love never fails" (1 Cor 13:7).

A true understanding of spiritual gifts perceives that they are simply God's love languages. Like a study by Gary Chapman, which defines the five love languages of humans, God also expresses love in many different ways and forms. Sometimes He expresses his love through a word aptly spoken that no human mind could have conceived (Prv 25:11). Sometimes He expresses his love by performing miraculous deeds or healing a sick person. At still other times He expresses his love by empowering human hands and feet to carry the message of the Cross to a lost and dying world.

Everything God does is motivated by love. First John 4:16 states that God is love. Love is the essence of his divine nature, and as that nature comes alive in us through the Holy Spirit, so will love become our nature. The Bible says in 1 John 4:19 that we are enabled to love because He first loved us. Out of our wealth, we give to others. This is precisely what the woman at the well did. With all the innocence of a child, she ran back to the town and spilled forth the living water with which, only moments prior, Jesus had quenched her own lifelong thirst.

For study, I have listed some additional Scriptures that detail different gifts and their function within the Body. I have also encouraged you to look up some passages that describe the Holy Spirit and his work as the third member of the Trinity. Finally, for reflection, there are some probing questions to help you discover your office and/or service at this season of life within your own local church body.

Scripture Study

Read John 4:19–30, 39–42.

1. How does the woman at the well respond when Jesus tells her that He is the Messiah?

2. When the disciples return, what two things does she do?

3. What spiritual gifts does this woman exercise?

Read 1 Corinthians 12–14 and answer the following questions:

1. List the gifts described in 12:8–10 and the offices listed in 12:28.

2. What does Paul repeatedly emphasize throughout this chapter about unity? What analogy does he use to make this point clearer?

3. How does understanding spiritual gifts as expressions of God's love safeguard us from error when using them?

4. How does the relationship between love and spiritual gifts relate to the concepts of worship in spirit and truth, which we studied in the last chapter?

5. How is God's definition of love (Chapter 13) different from the world's?

6. What does Paul say in Chapter 14 about placing too much emphasis on tongues rather than the other gifts, such as prophesy? Does this apply to your life? Are you placing too much emphasis on a particular gift or requirement?

7. What spiritual gifts have you witnessed being used in your local church? What gifts are not being used? Why do you think that is?

Read Joel 2:28–29. How does this prophecy apply to the end times Church, and particularly to women? Now look up the following verses: Acts 1:6–9; Acts 2:1–21, 37–41; Acts 4:33–35; Acts 6:7–8; Acts 19:17–20.

1. List the evidences of the Spirit being "poured out" in an individual's life and within the Church.

2. Are these things present in your life? In your church? If not, why?

3. What hindrances need to be removed for the Spirit to be released more in your life?

Read 2 Kings 4:1–7.

1. What does oil represent in the Bible?

2. What was the widow's responsibility in the fulfillment of this miracle?

3. What do the vessels represent?

4. What does this story suggest about the extent to which the Holy Spirit is "poured out" in our lives and churches?

Now read 1 Kings 17:10–16.

1. Again, what does the oil represent in this story?

2. What is significant about God's promise to the widow?

3. What does this promise represent to us?

4. What does this story suggest about spiritual gifts (compare with 1 Cor 13:8–13)? How can the oil in both widows' stories be compared to the "springs of living water" discussed in John 4:10–14?

Reflection

Set aside some time to spend in quiet reflection before God. Ask the Holy Spirit to help you complete the following (in your journal):

At this season of my life, God wants to express his love through me in these gifts/areas:

1.

2.

3.

I can exercise these gifts
1. At home by:

2. At church by:

3. And in outreach to hurting or unsaved people by:

In addition to recognizing your primary spiritual gifts, it is helpful to identify what groups of people to whom you feel most drawn. With that in mind, answer the following questions:
1. What age group do you most prefer to work with?

2. Do you enjoy working with males, females, or both?

3. How much experience have you had working with the age group you prefer?

4. How could you gain more experience?

Ask the Lord to reveal what his will is for your life in this season. Ask him to tell to you where and how He desires for you to exercise the gifts He has given you.

You may want to consider fasting as you seek this counsel from God. Whole or partial fasting sensitizes our hearts to hear God's voice more clearly. It also helps us focus and pray more effectively over time. If you have never received instruction on fasting, I recommend that you speak with your pastor before beginning a fast and seek additional resources on fasting from your Church library or Christian bookstore.

Also, if you struggle to identify your spiritual giftings, you may want to purchase a spirituals gifts test from your local Christian bookstore. These tests can serve as a good starting point. Ask your friends and family what they see as your particular strengths. Above all, I encourage you to be open to the Spirit's leading and patiently continue to seek and serve him with the opportunities you're given.

Released for
Ministry

10

In verse 25 of John 4, the woman at the well cries out, "I know that Messiah (called Christ) is coming. When he comes, he will explain everything to us." Jesus follows her statement with one of Scripture's finest phrases: "I who speak to you am he." Such authority in those elegant words! Even their rolling cadence suggests the lifting of the mighty veil. For a brief moment, the Divine Husband reveals himself intimately to his unsuspecting Bride.

I can only imagine the thoughts that raced through the Samaritan woman's mind as she gazed upon the unveiled Son of God. I can only dream what joy began to dawn across the dark horizon of her broken heart. What hope, what longing, what gratitude and unbridled love she must have felt charging her senses. In one incredible moment, she met Jesus face-to-face in an intimacy which only a handful of believers ever realized while He was in the flesh. He bared himself to her just as she had allowed him to lay bare her life before him.

With few exchanged words, an encounter takes place between Jesus and the woman at the well much like that which occurred between Boaz and Ruth in Ruth 3:7–15. Not knowing who Jesus was, the woman states her faith that someday the Messiah would answer the nagging questions of her disillusioned life. He would meet her needs for understanding and, by implication, much more. Although she had little basis for this hope, the Samaritan woman believed that Messiah, called Christ, would become for her a kinsman-redeemer, much like Ruth sought in Boaz. When Ruth uncovered Boaz's feet and lay down beside him, she sought his protection in marriage from the desolation and bleak future of her widowhood. When Boaz awoke, he told Ruth, "Don't be afraid. I will do for you all that you ask" (v. 11). When Jesus replies to the woman at the well, He essentially promises the same thing to her which Boaz assured Ruth. With words of sweet simplicity, Jesus lifts the veil of his identity and extends this garment of protection and blessing over her. He assures her, "I who speak to you am He."

Then, in the midst of this spiritual embrace, something disconcerting happens. The disciples show up (Jn 4:27). Funny how it always seems to happen that way. In a moment of intense intimacy with the Lord, the doorbell rings—or the baby wakes up, or your good friend fails to understand, let alone share, your excitement over God's newest work in your life. Or maybe it's worse. For example, your marriage may take a bad turn immediately following a spiritual retreat during which you experienced great personal breakthrough. Or your boss calls you in to let you know your job is on the line. All of these events constitute experiences of what I call the "collision with the natural."

This strange but familiar phenomenon is well documented throughout Scripture. It seems there is a common pattern that accompanies the advance of God's kingdom on earth and in individual lives. Immediately following spiritual breakthroughs come very "natural" tests. Some call it warfare, and certainly that reality cannot be denied. However, a closer look at these experiences reveals a greater purpose behind them.

Take the Samaritan woman's case, for example. Her "collision with the natural" occurs when the disciples show up at what would seem to be the worst possible time. Things get a little awkward as everyone wonders why Jesus is talking to this Samaritan woman. No one dares to ask questions, but their inquiries scream out through the uncomfortable silence. The woman lingers for a moment, lost in the love and holiness emanating from the eyes of her undisturbed Savior. She is torn; she wants to stay with him, but something pressures her to leave. She is faced with a choice.

A close study of other scriptural "collisions" suggest that all such encounters lead to an inevitable place of decision-making. For example, in 1 Kings 19, Elijah flees from Jezebel only one day after witnessing the Lord's miraculous judgment of 400 prophets of Baal. Literally hours after experiencing holy fire from heaven (1 Kgs 18), Elijah collides with overwhelming "natural" needs and fears; as a result, he runs into the desert and cries out to God (v. 3–4).

Understanding the purpose of such "collisions" helps us to be merciful to those, including ourselves, who occasionally experience them. Rather than rebuke Elijah for overreacting to Jezebel's threat, the Lord sends an angel to provide for Elijah both nourishment and rest (v. 5–8). Then, after forty days of physical recuperation, God invites Elijah to discuss the matter (v. 9–18). Elijah's response to

Jezebel, his collision experience, caused him to flee from God's appointed call upon his life. However, God is merciful and transforms this failure into an opportunity to further define his will and strategy for Elijah's task. He assigns Elijah some help and musters the forces for a second attack (v. 15–21).

Another collision encounter fits well here. In Matthew 26, immediately following the Last Supper, Jesus warns Peter that a collision with the natural is drawing near. For several days during the Passover festival, the disciples enjoyed tremendous favor and popularity among the people. Not only that, but they experienced highly intimate encounters with Jesus, culminating in the Last Supper. Suddenly, the tide turns. In the garden of Gethsemane, Judas initiates Christ's betrayal into the hands of men. Peter wants desperately to follow, but he is afraid.

Christ forewarned Peter that Peter would deny knowing Christ three times before dawn (v. 33–35). Peter argued vehemently that he was ready to die if necessary to follow Christ. Peter's spirit was willing, but his flesh was weak (Mt 26:41). When the natural threat of similar persecution came upon Peter, he retreated in fear. Three times he failed the collision test.

Once again, God does not rebuke man's failure to survive the natural onslaught. Instead, Christ makes a special point to inform, meet with, and reinstate Peter following the Resurrection (Mk16:7). Rather than add to his defeat, the Lord uses Peter's failure to teach him and further define the calling upon his life (Jn 21:7–20).

Collisions with the natural occur regularly throughout Scripture. They aren't pretty, but they serve a definite purpose in God's plan for the corporate and personal restoration of his people. As we have seen, these experiences lead us to a place of decision—a choice whether to continue on with God or to retreat. Our decisions in these encounters reveal the strength of our hearts for actual obedience. Thus, collisions serve to test and refine our passion for Jesus.

When the woman at the well faced the disciples' untimely return, she had a choice. She could slip away quietly and try to forget this unusual rabbi, or she could embrace his invitation and believe He was the Messiah. Unlike Elijah and Peter, the Samaritan woman does not retreat. Even though she leaves the well, she runs back to the town and immediately begins to testify. Verse 28 says she left her water jar (representing natural or past resources) and ran back to town saying, "Is not this the Christ?" (v. 29, KJV) The woman at the well faces the collision and overcomes.

While it is wonderful to experience intimate encounters with Jesus Christ, the real test of restoration comes when we return to daily life. We cannot tell how much we've grown until we collide with the natural to see who wins. Like two beefy football players, we must attack head on and see who falls down first. Collision experiences come when we "leave the mountain" and return to life on earth, which may not be "as it is in heaven" (Mt 6:10). These experiences aren't fun, but they represent a crucial element of life on earth.

In Mark 9:1–10, Jesus takes Peter, James, and John up a high mountain where He is transfigured before them. The Scriptures tell us that his clothes became dazzling white as He stood before them talking with Moses and Elijah (v. 3–4). This must have been an awesome experience, to say the least, one the disciples would never forget. In the midst of this overwhelming encounter, Peter tells Jesus, "Rabbi, it is good for us to be here. Let us put up three shelters—one for you, one for Moses, and one for Elijah" (v. 5).

Peter's request is understandable; it is one many of us have expressed at some point during our walk with God. We discover such a beautiful place of intimacy, knowledge, or ministry that we don't ever want to leave. We want to stay right where we are forever. In one such place, I remember telling God, "You go on and march with time, but I'm going to sit here for a while and have a picnic." I remember other times when I praised God that time continued whether I felt like I could go on or not. In those days, it was a comfort to know that even if dragged along by the neck, I would get through those experiences. There are days when time is our friend and others, our foe.

In the sweet places of new discovery, we are tempted to become like spiritual drunks, so caught up in the wine of God's precious Spirit that we forget about the rest of the world, whom Christ also came to save. Like Peter we exclaim, "It's good for us to be here.

Let's pitch a tent!" Jesus's response, or lack thereof, is significant. The scene simply changes, and the disciples come down from the mountain. As long as the earth exists, we will forever be "coming down the mountain." In other words, the collisions with the natural that we experience on this side of heaven represent our daily fare. Why? First of all, because these experiences serve to refine the work of God in our lives. They challenge and process the inner work of the Spirit into an outer witness and representation of Christ through our lives. Secondly, we will face daily collisions because God loves lost people, and He eagerly desires to work through us in finding them (2 Pt 3:9). We are his natural hands and feet, even while being supernaturally transformed to his heart. This is why Jesus prayed in John 17: "My prayer is not that you take them out of the world, but that you protect them from the evil one ... As you have sent me into the world, I have sent them into the world" (v. 15,18).

Our response to the collision with the natural determines the progress of God's work in our lives. Moreover, these experiences prepare us to be released in ministry. As stated previously, natural collisions test the strength of our hearts for actual obedience. Like a penetrating searchlight, they reveal our true character and the extent to which that character lines up with Christ. In the story of the rich young ruler (Lk 18:18–27), Jesus challenges this disciple to confront how wealth was inhibiting his spiritual growth. Not to suggest that prosperity is bad, but in this man's case, money had become a stumbling block.

Luke 18:23–25 records, "When he heard this, he became very sad, because he was a man of great wealth. Jesus looked at him and said, 'How hard it is for the rich to enter the kingdom of God! Indeed it is easier for a camel to go through the eye of a needle than for a rich man to enter the kingdom of God.'" According to certain commentaries, a "camel going through the eye of a needle" referred to the process whereby a loaded camel was taken through the narrow entrance of a palace courtyard. The only way for the camel to get through involved completely unloading all of the animal's burdens and forcing the camel to crawl through on its knees. The camel could get through, but the process took much time, energy, and cooperation from the camel. What an accurate picture of God's unloading of us!

When he came to Jesus, the rich young ruler had been serving God since his youth (Lk 18:21). He knew enough of God to desire more. Rather than receive him warmly, however, Christ encouraged him to count the cost (Lk 9:62). Jesus initiated a collision experience that forced the young man to process his desire into natural manifestations of godliness. Like passing meat through a meat grinder, Jesus sought to identify the real quality of the young man's heart. We all know the rest of the story. At least at this point in his life, the young ruler failed the collision test. He turned away.

In order to be released for ministry, we must know the true condition of our heart. God is a loving God. He does not wish to set us up where we will fail irreparably. Thus, He initiates practice tests everyday through which we can keep a record of the changes taking place in our hearts and the growing passion level which prepares us for ministry. As Mike Bickle reiterates throughout *Passion for Jesus*, only passion will keep us from the boredom of religion. Passion alone has the power to ignite our hearts and set ablaze our ministries for Christ. Our pursuit of his Person, our expression of his intimacy, our manifestation of the joy of his Presence, will draw the world to seek his face. No amount of fancy programming, persuasive speeches, or threatening appeals will invite the conversion of the lost like a soul who has been radically transformed by consuming love for Jesus.

The woman at the well faced an awkward collision when the disciples returned. Still swooning in spiritual fervor, she made a decision. She had been forgiven much, and she loved much (Lk 7:47). She was not about to let Christ slip away from her heart. He was the Messiah who had explained all things to her and about her (Jn 4:25, 29). The fire of his touch had so warmed her heart that she immediately felt compelled to share it with someone. Thus, she leaves her water jar and runs back to town with the springs of eternal life now bursting forth from within her.

Our release for ministry often depends on our successful navigation of natural collisions. In those incidences, whatever form they take, we must choose to walk in the Spirit and not the flesh

(Gal 5:16). Though we face war, we must walk in peace. Though we face hate, we must walk in love. Though we face disturbances and overwhelming circumstances of every kind, we must insist on faith. The most important thing to realize when confronting collisions of the natural is this: We choose the outcome. God's Spirit is a spirit of peace, of love, and of a sound mind (2 Tm 1:7). When we give in to anything else, He will temporarily withdraw (Sg 3:1–3). If we want to continue in whatever nearness or breakthrough we have recently received, we must refuse to *react* and opt instead to appropriately *respond*.

This is what the woman at the well did. When the disciples returned, she did not react to them. In fact, she never uttered a single word. Instead, she made a choice. She let go of the well and embraced the spring (Jn 4:13-14). As a result, she was released for ministry, and God used her to evangelize her entire village. When we learn to successfully navigate our collisions with the natural, choosing to hang on to Christ no matter what it takes, we, too, can experience the joy and power of ministering to others. As the waters of God's Holy Spirit pass through our lives to nourish others, we will experience new levels of restoration. Our lives will become as the stirring waters of Bethesda (Jn 5:4), a pool of healing and encouragement for a world maimed by sin.

Scripture Study

Begin by reviewing John 4:25–42. For now we will skip over the embedded metaphors of food and harvest in verses 31–38. Let's focus instead on three significant "events" in Scene 4. The first one is "the collision with the natural."

1. Describe a time when you experienced a collision with the natural. What preceded your collision? How did you respond?

2. How were you tested through that experience? Did you pass the test? What did you learn?

Turn to the story of Elijah in 1 Kings 19:1–17.

1. What sort of collision does Elijah face?

2. How does understanding "the collision of the natural" help you explain Elijah's exaggerated response first to Jezebel and then to the Lord?

3. What other factors may have caused Elijah to flee? (Hint: Notice how God meets him and provides for him). What does this suggest about our readiness to face collision experiences?

4. When are we most likely to flee and fail the test?

Look also at Exodus 32: 7–20.

1. How does Moses respond when he comes down from the mountain?

2. How does this compare to experiences you have had with other people or yourself following mountaintop encounters with God?

Read Mark 9:1–10.

1. Why does Peter ask the Lord if they could build three tents?

2. Have you ever wanted to "camp out" at a certain place with God?

3. How does Jesus respond?

4. Why is it necessary for us to return to the natural following such intense spiritual experiences?

5. Is it only for others' sakes that we return?

6. What might happen to us if we never came off the mountain? Are you ready to stay permanently on the mountain?

When we collide with the natural, we are presented with an inevitable choice (the second major event of Scene 4).

7. What is that choice?

Read again John 4:27–29.

1. What choice does the woman make?

2. How do you know?

The third event in this final scene is the "release for ministry" which always follows "the choice." Release for ministry represents the final stage of the upward cycle of restoration.

1. How do we know this woman has been restored?

2. What is the result of her being "released for ministry"?

Reflection

In your journal, record some of the ways you have experienced "collisions with the natural." In the past, how have you handled these circumstances? What can you learn from your own mistakes? How does understanding the "collision" process help you face these circumstances more effectively?

Are you willing to be released for ministry? What inhibitions or questions do you have with regard to going forward with God, whatever that may mean in your life?

How can our unwillingness to be released into ministry inhibit the flow of God's Spirit through our lives?

Have you ever experienced this, or have you seen this in others around you? What would you say to someone struggling in this area?

In what areas do you feel you still need to grow before being released to minister? What does the word "ministry" mean to you?

Returning Home

11

In the last lesson, we began to study the fourth scene of the woman at the well, the release for ministry. We discussed the three events of this scene that lead to every woman's similar release: the collision with the natural, the choice, and the release.

This chapter further addresses the concept of women and ministry, a controversial yet timely topic. If we truly believe, as the Samaritan woman's story affirms, that the end goal of God's restorative efforts in our lives involves being released to participate in the restoration of others, then we must address what is the proper role of women in Christian ministry.

As with other issues in this study, I wish to begin by orienting us within the framing text of John 4. In verse 28, the woman at the well leaves her water jar, which symbolized her own resources, and ran back to the town where she testified extensively concerning Jesus. Her testimony proved to be so powerful that it won the attention, and even conversion, of many in that town. Few of her actual words are recorded, but the impact of those words rings clear. God anointed her to take that city by storm.

Women in ministry have long been a thorn in the Church's side. In light of the wealth of scriptural precedent for women in ministry which the Bible affords, I am not sure why. In both the Old and New Testaments, women supplied nearly every role within the Church. Deborah served as judge; Bathsheba as queen mother; Esther as intercessor; Anna and Mary of Bethany as prophets; Mary Magdalene as evangelist; Priscilla as teacher; and Phoebe as apostle or deaconess, just to name a few. Women supported Jesus's ministry through their finances, hospitality, prayers, prophetic acts, and worship—and He didn't seem to have a problem with any of it, even when his disciples did (Mt 26:6–13). In fact, Jesus regularly elevated women's status by entrusting them with privileged information and relationships with him despite social and religious opposition.

Truly, our Lord had a special compassion for women, which He displayed consistently throughout his ministry on earth. This compassion fills the story of the woman at the well, which I believe prophetically details God's plan for the restoration of all women. As we have seen in previous chapters, this plan involves several different stages beginning with the surrender of self, followed by healing from the past and entering relationship with God through intimate worship. The final stage of this process, which we began to study in the last chapter, involves being released for ministry. This process of release is doubly necessary for women.

First, it is necessary for personal growth. There comes a point in our walk with God when we must accept the call to ministry lest we run the risk of becoming spiritual "fat babies." As Paul tells the Corinthians in 1 Corinthians 3:2–3, only the milk of the Word is suitable for those who are babes in their faith and understanding, while the meat of the Word is reserved for those who are more mature. In his letter, Paul chastises the Corinthians for remaining too long on mere "milk," when they should have been maturing to greater levels of service and sacrifice. Their selfishness and unwillingness to "grow up" caused a multitude of problems within the Church of Corinth, including controversies, divisions, and immoral activities. Being released in ministry to others encourages us to grow up in Christ. It challenges us to work out our salvation to its complete end in God (Phil 2:12).

Secondly, women need to be released for ministry to complete God's purpose for and through the Church. In Genesis 1:26–27, God said: "Let us make man in our image, in our likeness, and let *them* rule over the fish of the sea and the birds of the air, over the livestock, over all the earth, and over all the creatures that move along the ground. So God created man in his own image, in the image of God he created them; *male and female he created them.*" There has been much destructive teaching over the years which suggests that women were somehow made as an afterthought, as though God looked at Adam when it was all said and done and thought—"That boy's gonna need someone to take care of him!" One rib later and boom! Out came Eve. This teaching would further suggest that woman became man's stumbling block more than his help, forever suspect, highly fallible, and never ever to be entrusted with any real responsibility.

Thus, what God created to be the perfect union and representation of his image—man *and* woman—became pitted against each other almost from the beginning. Truly, Satan knew what he was doing when he deceived Eve in the garden. Thankfully, God knew, too, and already had a plan—a plan in which we, as women of the final ages, play a vital part.

Sometimes I think God just likes a good challenge and that's why He tolerates Satan. When the Lord addressed Satan after the Fall, He said, "I will put enmity between you and the woman, and between your offspring and hers; he will crush your head, and you will strike his heel. To the woman [God] said, 'I will greatly increase your pains in childbearing; with pain you will give birth to your children. Your desire will be for your husband, and he will rule over you.'"

For women, the Fall produced three major outcomes. The first outcome involves a God-ordained, mutual hatred between women and Satan. A woman, Eve, first recognized who Satan really was—a deceiver, and she exposed him (Gn 3:13). Adam blamed flesh and blood, but Eve discerned the spiritual perpetrator. Today women continue to be particularly attuned to discerning evil. They have been gifted by God to expose the enemy, and for that reason, Satan hates women. Not only that, but women have the unique capacity to host new life. They are birthers, both naturally and spiritually, of God's creative power.

The second major outcome for women from the Fall concerned childbearing. God said He would greatly increase women's pain in childbirth. Some have suggested that the pain to which God referred meant more than physical pain during labor and delivery. As many mothers would attest, the real pain of childbearing amounts to countless hours of worry and prayer as those children grow up and struggle to survive the world. Somehow, through this pain, God knew that women would be drawn back to dependency upon him and the redeeming power of the Blood of Christ.

Finally, the third outcome of the Fall occurred in the final sentence of Genesis 3:16, when God said to the woman, "Your desire shall be for your husband, and he will rule over you." This punishment has been felt by women all over the world throughout all ages. Women have a deep desire for intimacy and acceptance from men, particularly their fathers and husbands. This desire is God-given, central to our feminine makeup and ministry. At the same time, this attribute has been for women an Achilles' heel that the enemy strikes to cripple and destroy us. Our passion for intimacy drives us like an insatiable appetite and leaves us highly vulnerable to a variety of devastating setbacks.

Thousands of years later, we still experience daily the effects of the Fall in our relationships as men and women. Even the Church struggles to understand and accept what is the proper relationship of these two drastically different sexes in the ministry and representation of God to the world. In the garden, they were helpmates, equal partners in the care and administration of God's creation. But what about now? What about in the Church?

I know I am skating on thin ice, even when writing for women, so let me hasten to safer ground. The bottom line of the woman at the well story is this: Revival came to that town through a *woman*. When Jesus could have chosen anyone, male or female, to ignite the fire and start the church in Samaria, He called upon a woman to do so, and a broken, despised woman at that. God is no respecter of persons; He does not look at outer appearance but at the heart (1 Sm 16:7).

This was not the first, nor the last, time that God would choose a woman to initiate and proclaim something new. God used Mary, the mother of Jesus; Elizabeth, the mother of John the Baptist; and Anna to prophesy Christ's coming into the world (Lk 1; 2:36). Later, God chose Mary of Bethany to anoint Christ in keeping with the Old Testament prophetic act of anointing kings (Mk 14:3–9). Finally, upon his resurrection, Christ revealed himself initially only to women, thus establishing them as the first witnesses and evangelists of his resurrected glory. At the tomb He told them, "Do not be afraid. Go and tell my brothers … " (Mt 28:10).

Why did He appear to the women first? Perhaps for several different reasons. First of all, the women came to the tomb. On that early morning, most of the men were hiding in the upper room, afraid of further arrests and persecutions. The women could move about more freely because they did not pose the same threat to the Roman government. In many countries, this is still true; women can minister far more freely than men because their lower social status serves to camouflage their activities. Or maybe Christ was testing the men by appearing to women first. Would the men believe his Word, even if it came through a woman's testimony? In Roman society, women were not allowed to testify in court concerning any civil dispute. But would the men accept their spiritual testimony? Would the men receive them, as Jesus did, to be partners in ministry (Lk 8:1–3)?

For whatever reason, God Incarnate did choose to reveal his resurrected glory first to women, just as He chose to unveil himself in an unprecedented way to the Samaritan woman. She was only one of a handful of people to whom Christ openly identified himself before the Resurrection. Many people asked the question, "Are you the One?" but Jesus rarely gave them as straight an answer as He did the woman at the well.

I don't know why God chose to use women in peculiar circumstances such as these any more than I understand why God continues to call out to women in similar situations today. What I do know is that, practically speaking, there are three issues that must be resolved in women's hearts before they can successfully embrace whatever ministry God makes available to them. All of these issues are represented in the story of the woman at the well. It is interesting that the same issues that applied to her thousands of years ago still affect modern women. Let us look at each of these issues individually.

The first issue to be resolved in women's hearts concerns the question of whether it is God's will for women to minister in corporate, church settings. For women to be effectively released in their gifts, they must settle this issue, once and for all, in their own hearts. This sounds much easier than it actually is. After all, there has been no lack of wrong and muddled teaching on this subject. I will not attempt to provide a definitive answer to the many questions that have been raised over women in the Church, but I would like to clarify what *is* and *is not* at issue.

Most arguments in favor of women's participation in church ministry simply cite the overwhelming number of women who reportedly held prominent positions throughout Israel's history

(Jgs 4:4) and within the early church (Acts 18; Rom 16:1, 3). Arguments against women's participation typically focus on two Scripture passages, both written by the apostle Paul. The first passage is found in 1 Corinthians 14:33–35, and states, "For God is not a God of disorder but of peace. As in all the congregations of the saints, women should remain silent in the churches. They are not allowed to speak, but must be in submission as the Law says. If they want to inquire about something, they should ask their own husbands at home; for it is disgraceful for a woman to speak in the church."

It must be remembered that at this time, the Church was still predominantly conducted according to Jewish temple practices, in which the priests or primary administrators would have been men. Thus, for a woman to speak out in church, she would have to interrupt church proceedings. Throughout 1 Corinthians, Paul's main objective involved correcting a wayward and prideful group of believers (1 Cor 5:18). The Corinthian church had enthusiasm for spiritual gifts, but lacked the maturity to know their proper place and function in worship (1 Cor 12:1). The Corinthian church leadership was struggling to maintain order among both men and women (1 Cor 1:11–13; 3:1–4; 5:1–2). I do not dismiss the application of this passage to modern believers, because I believe all Scripture is God-breathed and useful for instruction (2 Tm 3:16). However, understanding the time and context of Paul's letter to the church at Corinth offers insight into what otherwise might appear to be a serious inconsistency in Paul's teachings.

Specifically, in 1 Corinthians 11:13–15, Paul gives explicit instructions for how women were to pray and prophesy in public settings. So, three chapters later, his writings show that he obviously did not intend an absolute silence. In 1 Corinthians 11:11, Paul states, "In the Lord, woman is not independent of man, *nor is man independent of woman.*" This key verse suggests that Paul was well aware of the need for balance in ministry that included both men and women. Again, his concern was simply order. He wished to emphasize "a proper time and procedure for every matter" (Eccl 8:5). At that point in history, few women were sufficiently educated or knowledgeable of Scripture to speak with authority on religious matters. It is believed that many of the women's "interruptions" in church involved simple questions that their husbands could more easily and properly answer at home. When Paul admonishes the women and men to discuss these matters at home, I believe that he is actually encouraging the men to bring their wives up to speed with regard to religious education so that they could pray and prophesy in corporate prayer meetings whenever the Spirit gave them utterance to do so (Acts 2:4).

A second controversial passage appears in 1 Timothy 2:11–15. In this passage, Paul writes to his young protégé, Timothy: "A woman should learn in quietness and full submission. I do not permit a woman to teach or to have authority over a man; she must be silent" (v. 11–12). Paul then goes on to explain that man was formed first and woman deceived first. He concludes by saying "But women will be saved through childbearing—if they continue in faith, love and holiness with propriety." Again, context is significant—both historically and textually—not to dismiss the passage but to shed light on its true meaning. Historically, there were very few women at that time who had sufficient education and/or religious training to teach. It is also believed that many women in Ephesus (the location of Timothy's congregation), like Corinth, had adopted a rebellious attitude, which needed correction. Similar to many feminists of modern society, it appears to historians that these women were out to conquer men, not find their place alongside them.

Within the greater text of 1 Timothy, this passage, like that in 1 Corinthians, serves to provide guidelines for orderly worship. In both cases, Paul's overriding concern involves order, not oppression. He is not out to shut down the Holy Spirit or his gifts in any part of the Body (1 Cor 12:12). Rather, he provides practical teaching for the exercise of gifts and offices within the Church.

I do not believe Paul intended to deny women their proper place within the Church. In some ways, he spoke to the times and circumstances in which he lived and served. Greek women had much in common with modern women. They desired to be released in their gifts, but they had many misunderstandings which prompted them to adopt the rebellious and ungodly ways of women in the world (1 Cor 11:12–18; 1 Tm 2:9). Paul's instructions to Timothy regarding women in leadership do not impose any limitations that he did not similarly prescribe for men (1 Tm 3:1–13). If men or women did not have their own houses in order, they were not to exercise authority in the church. Both men and women were required to submit to proper authorities and conduct godly lives in public and private realms, so that "no one will malign the word of God" (Ti 2:5).

The first issue that every woman must settle within herself before experiencing significant release in ministry involves whether or not it really is God's will for women to minister—whatever that means to them. One of the greatest passages from Jesus's own life that speaks to this issue occurs in Luke 13:10–17. On the Sabbath, Jesus was teaching in the synagogue when He became aware of a woman who was afflicted with a degenerative bone disorder. For eighteen years, she had not been able to see the sun or even look people in the eye when speaking with them. Jesus had compassion for her and, before the people, cried out, "Woman, thou art loosed ... And he laid his hands on her: and immediately she was made straight, and glorified God" (v. 12-13, KJV).

Rather than rejoice at her healing, the religious leaders became indignant. I wonder whether they were more perturbed because the healing occurred on the Sabbath, because it happened to a woman, or simply because Jesus did something that they could not imitate. In any case, the Pharisees and Sadducees did not approve of Jesus's habitual practice of displacing religious tradition. Many people in the church today possess the same attitude.

Jesus responds to their indignation in an even more forceful manner when He calls them hypocrites and addresses the woman as a "daughter of Abraham." By using this form of address, Jesus establishes that she has equal rights to the claims and inheritance of God's promise to Abraham. This promise included prosperity and blessing "for all nations through your descendants" as well as complete possession of the land of promise (Gn 17:8; 18:18). In his day and age, Jesus's proclamation of this promise to a woman rattled some cages among the Jews. It was a bold statement, in keeping with his earlier words, "Woman, thou art loosed ..."

As I mentioned at the beginning of this lesson, women have successfully served in nearly every position within the Church, during both the Old and New Testaments. Since then, there have been countless others who have given their lives for the cause of Christ in any number of capacities. I believe that the bottom line regarding women in ministry is this: God can and will use women to fulfill the needs of his Church and the ongoing purposes of his mission to save the lost people—especially when a suitable or willing man cannot be found. Biblical precedent would suggest that God does prefer to use men to fill the primary *administrative* functions within the Church, probably because, on the whole, men are more naturally inclined to perform these duties. However, we should realize that God can and will use women if circumstances so dictate.

One of the greatest things we can learn from Paul's admonitions concerning the women of his day is this: We as women must carefully search our motives for desiring positions within the Church. Are we seeking to glorify God and support his Body, or do we have an alternate, and perhaps worldly influenced, agenda to usurp male authority? After all, our being restored to ministry in public spheres should not in any way threaten or compromise the ministry of men. Rather, in keeping with God's original design in Genesis, our return to ministry should complete and help the work of men. As Paul so aptly reminds us, men were created first, and we were created to assist and serve the work of God that began in and through them. Before we can truly be released into all God offers to us as women, we must be certain that we have rid our hearts of any impurity or nagging doubts that question the sovereign authority of God's will for our lives.

A second issue that must be resolved in women's hearts before they can function effectively in ministry concerns past abuses against women, and especially ministering women. When the woman at the well turned to depart from Jesus and return to the village, she had already settled two things in her heart: that Jesus would not have a problem with her being released to witness for him, and that she would forgive the abuses of the past. As she approached the townspeople, the woman was forced to overcome their past rejection of her. She had to forsake worrying about whether they would laugh at her or despise her again as in times past. She had to avoid any comparison of this day to her previous experiences in order for her to do what she felt called to do. In the end, she overcame all reservations and witnessed freely to the very people who had likely caused the majority of ridicule and rejection in her life.

For women to be released in ministry, we must get over the past. Not only must we forgive our offenders, but we must abandon all assumptions that this time will be like those occasions in the past when we may have attempted to exercise our gifts with poor, or even disastrous, results. In Exodus 3, when the Lord called Moses to present himself before Pharaoh and lead the children of Israel out of Egypt, Moses fought hard to refuse. He came up with a slew of good-sounding excuses, most of which were entirely untrue.

Moses tried every loophole, finally claiming in Exodus 4:10, "I have never been eloquent … I am slow of speech and tongue." In essence, Moses tried to persuade the Lord that he was a nobody, that no one would believe him, and that God should really send someone else. For a time, the Lord was patient, but near the end He became agitated with Moses. After all, there was no one more prepared than Moses to lead Israel at that time. Moses had been raised in the palace, among the Egyptian nobles, and educated in Egyptian schools. No one in all Israel had the knowledge of Pharaoh or the Egyptians that Moses had. Most likely, Moses was formally trained in public speaking, even if he didn't consider himself a gifted orator. Furthermore, even before he left Egypt the first time, Moses had already been recognized as a leader among both the Egyptians and the Jews.

The real problem lay in Moses's past. Behind all his excuses, Moses was being held captive by a murderous accusation from the past. Something deep within him recoiled at the thought of returning to the site of his earlier failures. Simply stated, he had no reason to believe things would be any different. Before, the Jews had rejected him (Ex 2:14). Before, the Egyptians had threatened his life (Ex 2:15). Why should it be any different this time?

Many women today are deeply afraid of failure and of being rejected or ridiculed once again. Many of us bear the wounds of traumatic pasts in which the things of God, the deepest spiritual gifts and dreams within us, were aborted in our lives. Maybe we, like Moses, failed miserably. Maybe we, too, would prefer to stay on the safe side of the desert than answer God's call and risk what we have worked so hard to attain—respectability, status, and some measure of security. But, there is a world out there that needs deliverance. God is seeking willing servants who will go and lead them out. For us to be released in this mission, however, we must face our fears, our accusers, and our past failures. This is what the woman at the well had to do when she ran back to the town. Good news! She overcame them (Rv 12:11).

The final issue that must be resolved for women to be released in ministry is that we, like the Samaritan woman, must return home. When she left Jesus's side, the woman at the well did not consider all the distant places to which she could have gone to spread the Gospel. She didn't seek out the nearest synagogue or pulpit. She simply returned home. Under the influence of society and particularly feminist ideology, many women today have left home—if not physically, then emotionally and spiritually. The first step to many women's restoration in ministry may involve an invitation to return home and embrace the fullness of femininity as God has so beautifully orchestrated it. Our femininity runs deeper than physical attributes and the ability to host new life. Women are uniquely gifted as spiritual creatures to display the image of God, together with men.

One of the greatest deceptions of this age and deterrents to women being received in ministry has come from the modern feminist movement's promotion of gender blending. The liberation of women will not come from any dilution of male and female identities. Instead, this teaching promotes understandable hostility from men who in no way wish to be displaced. We in the Church are not competing for limited resources. There is plenty of work to go around, and plenty of blessing to share. Thus, we, as women, should not be primarily concerned about titles or positions of human design. If our hearts are pure, we will seek only to serve the Lord. Like our Samaritan sister, we will simply desire to tell the world, "Come see a Man who told me everything I ever did, everything I ever was, and everything I have been designed to be. Come and see … ."

It is time that we broaden our understanding of women and ministry. It is time we quit fighting to be like men and embrace being women. Our homes are our pulpits, our families our chorus, and our lives the most powerful sermon we could ever preach. Am I saying that women cannot serve in administrative or prominent positions within the Church? Absolutely not. Am I saying that all women should stay home and have babies in the hopes that their lives will somehow be redeemed with special anointing? Of course not, although it could happen. I am simply inviting my sisters in Christ to survey the battleground. Satan is conquering a lot of territory these days because the Church is too busy fighting within itself to organize a strategy against the enemy. And in case you haven't heard: Most lost people are in the world, not the Church. If we really want to be released in ministry, we have all the authority we need. No one is going to challenge us if we minister among the poor, the prostitutes, the battered wives, and battering mothers. Few will protest if we purpose to make our homes into havens again, places of refuge for the weary travelers of life such as our neighbors, loved ones, and even angels (Heb 13:2). Not even the demons of hell can prevail when we humble ourselves as servants among mankind in the likeness of Christ, and embrace the nurturing, creative strengths with which God has uniquely gifted women: gifts of prayer, intercession, warfare, hospitality, healing, and godly instruction.

The woman in Proverbs 31 possessed these gifts and many others. She even possessed gifts of administration which she applied to conduct business both within and outside her home (Prv 31:13–27). She was no weakling, but a serious force to be reckoned with. If we had more women like her, our communities, and churches, would be a lot healthier.

Queen Esther is another example of a godly woman released in her gifts. When faced with the potential destruction of her nation, she acted wisely, even shrewdly, to secure the will of God (Est 4:16–17). In that crucial hour, she did not lament or shun her femininity. Rather, she embraced her feminine gifts to win the favor of her king. In doing so, she successfully negotiated the salvation of many lives. She utilized gifts of prayer, fasting, intercession, hospitality, helps, and godly counsel. She displayed an exquisite sensitivity to the Lord's timing (Est 5:1–8; 7:1–6; 8:1–5). Truly, we would do well to follow her example in our own lives.

Women need to be released in ministry, both for their own sakes and for the well-being of the Church. Women possess unique spiritual sensitivities and contributions to complete the image of God in man. However, this release can only come when we lay to rest certain issues, doubts, grievances, and misconceptions from the past. Just like the Old Testament priests, we must be fully consecrated and cleansed before we are fit for service in the Temple. We must be especially wary of any organized feminist influence that will only bring strife into the Church. As God knows, *she* doesn't need any more strife. Let us, then, heed the call and return home—physically, emotionally, and spiritually as our circumstances dictate. Let us consecrate ourselves for the wonders of God:

> *And afterward, I will pour out my Spirit on all people. Your sons and daughters will prophesy, your old men will dream dreams, your young men will see visions. Even on my servants, both men and women, I will pour out my Spirit in those days. I will show wonders in the heavens and on the earth, blood and fire and billows of smoke… and everyone who calls on the Name of the Lord will be saved.*
>
> (Jl 2:28–30, 32a)

Scripture Study

In Lesson 10 we began to discuss the fourth scene of the woman at the well: the release for ministry.

1. List the three events from Scene 4 and how they relate to being "released."

2. In this lesson, we continued discussing what it means for women to be released in ministry. What are some of the issues which must be resolved in order for women to be released?

Read Genesis 3:6–19.

1. What are the three challenges that women face as a result of the Fall?

2. What do men face? How do these results account for many of our modern-day problems in marriage relationships?

3. Why does Satan despise women?

4. What, according to this passage, lies at the root of "women's intuition"? How have you found that to be true in your own life?

5. If you have children, how have the challenges of motherhood taught you a greater dependence on God?

Read Exodus 3:1–4:17.

1. List the excuses, in order, that Moses used to fend off God's call. Identify the false belief or untruth of each excuse.

2. How does God react when Moses asks him to send someone else? What can this teach us about our own resistance to God's will?

3. Have you ever argued with God? If yes, what was the real reason you didn't want to obey?

4. Do you have any "murderous accusations" from your past that come back to haunt you when you are faced with great opportunities or challenges?

Now turn to the Book of Esther. Read through this book if you are not already familiar with it. Look especially at Esther 4:12–5:8 and 7:1–8:5.

1. What did Mordecai ask Esther to do?

2. Who does Mordecai represent?

3. Who does Haman represent?

4. Who does the King represent?

5. List, in order, the steps Esther takes to prepare to go before the King. For each step, identify the spiritual parallel. What does this story teach us about being women of God?

Read Proverbs 31:10–31.

1. Describe some of the "ministries" of this woman.

2. What spiritual gifts are implied in this passage? Do you think the example this woman set applies today? If so, how are you doing?

Finally, read Joel 2:28–32 and Galatians 3:26–29.

1. What do these passages suggest about women in the Church? What does it mean to be a "prophesying daughter," "Abraham's seed," and an "heir of the promise"?

Reflection

Read 1 Corinthians 11:13–15, 14:33–35 and 1 Timothy 2:11–15. In your journal, write out your own explanation of these passages and what they mean for women.

Write your own "modern" version of the **Proverbs 31** description. What do you consider to be the defining characteristics of a godly woman?

Finally, answer the following questions:
1. What does it mean to you to be a "woman in ministry"?

2. What do you see as your role in the local church and/or community?

3. What issues do you still need to resolve? (Be sure to prayerfully commit these, in writing or out loud, to the Lord.)

4. In what ways, if any, do you need to return home?

Ripe for Harvest

12

As we conclude this study, let's tie up a few remaining loose ends. Specifically, in this lesson we will address two embedded analogies, or parables, which occur in the final verses of the Samaritan woman's story. Nothing in Scripture takes place by chance. Often the order and sequence of recorded Gospel events reveal as much about the heart of God as do the words used to relate them. Thus, it is no coincidence that Jesus relates these two analogies during the interim between the Samaritan woman's hasty departure and the return of the townspeople. The disciples have recently rejoined their Master, and Jesus grasps a teachable moment to instruct them in the heart of God.

The first analogy begins in John 4:31 when the disciples urge Jesus to eat. The Lord replies, "I have food to eat that you know nothing about" (v. 32). As you may remember, Jesus came to the site of Jacob's well and sat down because He was " tired from the journey" (v. 6). This must have been a strange feeling to an omnipotent God now confined, by his own will, to human limitations. When the disciples left to enter the town and purchase food, Jesus stayed behind supposedly to rest. Upon their return, they see that, once again, He has drawn a crowd for ministry (v. 30). Still not fully cognizant of who He was, the disciples urged Jesus to eat and regain his strength.

Their concern reminds me of the event in Matthew 12:47–50, when Mary, Jesus's mother, and his brothers called him to come outside so that they could speak with him. They were concerned about the personal strain of Jesus's growing ministry, not to mention the controversy and opposition that was also steadily increasing. Jesus responded to his family's request by saying, "'Who is my mother, and who are my brothers?' Pointing to his disciples, he said, 'Here are my mother and brothers. For whoever does the will of my Father in heaven is my brother and sister and mother.'"

Jesus's response in both cases is significant. On both occasions, He makes reference to the centrality of God's will in his life. In John 4:34, He even goes so far as to compare the will of God to the natural sustenance of food. Jesus states: "My food ... is to do the will of him who sent me and to finish his work." The disciples at this point are still grappling to differentiate between natural and supernatural (or spiritual) resources. Their minds remain largely bound to the things of this world, even as Jesus challenges them to let loose and see the bigger picture.

An interesting, albeit familiar, exchange ensues—much like the discourse shared by Jesus and the Samaritan woman in the early verses of this same chapter. We see the return of the interplay of natural and supernatural. As you may remember from Lesson 3 of this study, one of the key factors in Jesus's invitation to the woman at the well required an awakened sensitivity to supernatural, or spiritual, reality. In order for her to understand the truth of eternal life and the work of the Holy Spirit, she had to abandon her dependency upon mankind's wells and natural resources. She had to identify and respond to a deeper, spiritual thirst.

Now, in verses 33–34, Jesus strives to awaken a similar sensitivity among the disciples. This time the issue concerns food—natural food made by human hands—versus the spiritual food of God's will embodied in the life of his Son. Jesus said in John 5, "I tell you the truth, the Son can do nothing by himself, he can do only what he sees his Father doing, because whatever the Father does the Son also does ... By myself I can do nothing; I judge only as I hear, and my judgment is just, for I seek not to please myself but him who sent me" (v. 19, 30). When Jesus walked the earth, He purposed to live out the full will of God for the salvation of men (Mk 10:45) Philippians 2:7–8 states that Christ "emptied himself, taking the form of a bond-servant ... humbl[ing] Himself by becoming obedient to the point of death, even death on a cross." (NASB)

Jesus sets before the disciples a powerful example of what it means to live by faith. His heart is set to follow God at any cost; the sustenance He most desires to finish the work of God's will in and through his life. Some of you at this point may be tempted to think, "Yeah, well He was God. He could do that." However, Philippians 2 tells us that Jesus "did not regard equality with God a thing to be grasped, but emptied Himself" (v. 6-7, NASB). This means that Christ willingly gave up all rights to his divine nature during his earthly ministry. Not that He ceased to have these attributes, but He chose to relinquish them for a season (Mt 26:53–54).

In other words, although He was God, Jesus walked the earth with nothing more than you or I, through the Holy Spirit, might attain. Whatever insight, power or strength Jesus had He received from the Holy Spirit in the same manner which He made available to us through his death and resurrection.

Through his "food" analogy, Jesus encourages the disciples to realize there is more to life than meets the eye, or in this case, the tongue (Lk 12:22–26). Using the same manner with which He encouraged the Samaritan woman to drink living water, He now encourages the disciples to partake of the bread of life. Two chapters later, in John 6:35, Jesus declares, "I am the bread of life. He who comes to me will never go hungry, and he who believes in me will never be thirsty." Through these words, Jesus sought to prepare his disciples for a harvest they would soon begin to realize—the awesome task of building and maintaining God's Church. He challenged them to live by the Spirit and not the flesh (Gal 5:16,25), to seek the distant springs of supernatural sustenance rather than remain limited to what they could see, touch, taste, and feel.

Obviously, as long as we are clothed in flesh, we need to eat and sleep, and carry out all other necessary functions for human life. There is no spiritual gain in physical exhaustion. Christ did not intend to shame or condemn the disciples for seeking out food. In fact, it is likely He who told them to go into town and eat. By drawing their attention to other "food," Jesus simply encouraged them to keep their lives in perspective and remember that "man does not live by bread alone" but by the miraculous, sustaining will of God (Mt 4:4).

In essence, Jesus was introducing the disciples to a theme He would reiterate in greater detail throughout his ministry: the necessity of abiding. In preparation for the harvest (which his second analogy describes), Jesus emphasizes the preeminent truth of abiding for successful discipleship. In John 15:4, Jesus states: "Abide in Me, and I in you. As the branch cannot bear fruit of itself, unless it abides in the vine, so neither [can] you, unless you abide in Me" (NASB). Just as a branch cannot receive nourishment apart from the roots, neither can we sustain spiritual life apart from God. Even Jesus, God Incarnate, recognized his complete dependence upon the Father (Jn 5:19). We even more, must remain aware of our need.

To survive the harvest, we must learn to abide in Christ. We must daily draw our sustenance from roots driven deep into the truth of God's Word and the worship of his Spirit. Through the many disciplines of prayer, fasting, Bible study, worship, praise, and meditation, we must eat and drink the life of Christ daily (Jn 6:53–57). Our relationship to Christ must become so central to our lives that we, too, would say "My food is to do the will of Him who sent me."

One day as I was fasting, I thought about how easy it is to become dehydrated. After only one day without food or water, our bodies become weak, our minds fuzzy, and our hearts irritable from fatigue. As these thoughts passed through my mind, the Holy Spirit began to speak. He said,

> *You notice these things because they are visible. But don't you see that one day apart from God, without taking time to be fed and watered by his Word, will leave you spiritually dehydrated? You may not see it on the outside, but your spirit is weak, your discernment fuzzy, and your love waning.*

How often are you spiritually dehydrated? I know I am guilty of it even as I write this. Allowing ourselves to fall into this state is easy in a hectic world like ours. However, we, like the disciples, must learn to rely more on our spiritual well-being than our physical comfort. After all, the truth is—God can and will sustain us through all our natural needs (Mt 6:30–34).

What a stark contrast is laid out in these verses! The Samaritan woman, a mere babe in Christ, leaves behind her water jar and returns to tell the town about Jesus. She is no longer concerned primarily about the natural elements of physical life. She has experienced a powerful awakening of spiritual potential—a release of torrential love overflowing with such exuberance that the townspeople are drawn to investigate its source. On the other hand, the disciples return with arms loaded full of takeout bags and sticky fingers from too much fried fish. How well they are reflected in the conduct of the modern day church—having left behind the Savior to patronize the nearest fast food restaurant.

Before we can be entrusted with ministry, much less the great harvest of the last days (Mt 13:36–43), we must learn to rightly prioritize our time, talents, wants, and needs. We must not be running off to town every five minutes—putting our hand to the plow and forever looking back (Lk 9:62). We must move from a spirit of Martha to that of Mary, embracing the singularity of devotion that marked her ministry and worship "beautiful" in the sight of God (Mt 26:10; Mk 14:6).

This brings us to the second analogy. In John 4:35–38, Jesus asks the disciples:

> *Do you not say, 'Four months more and then the harvest'? I tell you, open your eyes and look at the fields! They are ripe for harvest. Even now the reaper draws his wages, even now he harvests the crop for eternal life, so that the sower and the reaper may be glad together. Thus the saying 'One sows and another reaps' is true. I sent you to reap what you have not worked for. Others have done the hard work, and you have reaped the benefits of their labor.*

I imagine Jesus said this as He watched the disappearing figure of the Samaritan woman, or perhaps He envisioned the responsive crowd. Further still, something within him gazed into the future to a time and day appointed by the Father when all whom He had chosen would return. In that momentary reverie, the heart of God cried out through the Son, expressing mingled concern and joy, saying: "Open your eyes—the harvest has begun!"

It is no secret we are living in the last days. I will not be surprised if Christ returns in my lifetime. In fact, I will be surprised if He doesn't. Two thousand years ago, our Savior stated that the fields were ripe for harvest. If the fields were ripe then, how much more they must be today! Revival is breaking out around the world. Millions are coming to Christ. The dead are being raised. the blind are seeing, the deaf are hearing, and the lame are walking. All over the world, the Lord of the harvest is dispensing his laborers (Lk 10:2).

America is one of the last countries to receive this tremendous move of God. Like the workers brought in at the final hour, our experience of the harvest has been limited (Mt 20:1–16). However, for the remnant we represent, God is faithful and He will surely not forget us (Is 49:15). In days ahead, I suspect America will see amazing displays of both God's judgment and grace. Both dread and joy of the Lord will cover our wounded, sinful land. When that time comes, and actually has now come (Jn 4:21), we need to be ready—restored to full working capacity and able to receive the harvest of lost souls.

As I emphasized at the beginning of this lesson, nothing in Scripture occurs by chance. It is no coincidence that these two analogies take place within the larger framework of the woman-at-the-well-account. Her story relates the pathway to restoration for women and, ultimately, for the Church. She represents a symbol of the reunited, restored Church—part Jew, part Gentile, including all nations, races, genders, and socioeconomic classes. In God, there are no outcasts—only those who have cast him out.

These two analogies define what is to be the "abiding purpose" of every believer. Our heritage as the Bride of Christ involves being willing to partake of the same bread and cup from which our Lord derived his life on earth. In Luke 19:10 Jesus declares, "For the Son of Man came to seek and save what was lost." This verse encapsulates the mission of Jesus Christ. He came not to condemn the world but to save and restore all those who would receive him (Jn 3:17).

Acts 3:21 states that Christ shall be held back in heaven "until the time when God will restore everything." In lesson 11, we studied the Fall of man and the many implications of the Fall for men, women, and all of creation (Gn 3). As the return of Christ approaches, we should expect to see the world turned "right side up" with restoration occurring on many levels and with many different types of relationships. We should anticipate the return of many people to the Lord and the restoration of all believers as the Holy Spirit prepares the Bride to meet her Bridegroom (Rv 19:7–8).

As Isaiah 61:4 promises, we shall witness the rebuilding of "ancient ruins," and the renewal of that which has been "devastated for generations." The house of God will be set in order—the Body of Christ resurrected cell by cell, member by member, one life at a time. This is the message underlying the story of the woman at the well. Our God is a God of personal restoration. No matter what measure of devastation the enemy has wrought in our lives, families, or even ministries, Jesus Christ has the power to bind up the brokenhearted and save those who are crushed in spirit (Ps 34:18). Above all, He is faithful, and He will keep his promise to bless all nations as the seed of Abraham fulfills its harvest (Gn 26:4).

John 4:39–42 records the result of Jesus's harvest in the Samaritan village of Sychar. Verse 39 states "Many of the Samaritans of that town believed in him because of the woman's testimony." Many people converted immediately simply on account of the woman at the well. Still others urged Christ to stay with them, and He did for two more days. His words convinced even more individuals to join in, and a fellowship of believers was established (v. 41–42).

Thus, our story draws to a close. The woman is restored. No longer is she outcast, broken, or despised. Following her brief encounter with Jesus, the woman becomes situated as an evangelist of the best news ever told. The church of Samaria is born through her broken body and the anointing of God that spilled forth. The town of Sychar will never be the same.

Before signing off, let's take a look at one final account of another woman's restoration: Ruth the Moabitess. Ruth lived during the time of the Judges, a dark period in Israel's history. She married into a Jewish family that had moved to Moab hoping to escape the famine in Israel. After a while, Ruth's husband, Mahlon, died, along with her father-in-law and brother-in-law, leaving three women to fend for themselves in already depressed economic times.

Naomi, Ruth's mother-in-law, decides to return home. Though bitterly disappointed with life, Naomi is a godly woman and knows that her husband's decision to leave the land of God was not wise and possibly accounted for his death and that of his sons. In the midst of her grief, Naomi determines to fall into the hands of God and obey the leading of her heart (Ru 1:6). Ruth decides to accompany her despite Naomi's strict warning of the possible rejection that Ruth, a Moabitess, might face in Israel. After all, Mosaic law at the time forbade Moabites from entering the temple of God for ten generations (Deut 23:3).

Still, Ruth sets her heart to follow Naomi. In fact, she takes a vow that nothing but death should separate them. She declares: "Where you go, I will go and where you stay, I will stay. Your people will be my people and your God will be my God" (Ru 1:16).

Back in Israel, life proves to be a challenge for the two widows. In order to provide food for them, Ruth becomes a gleaner in the harvest fields. She follows along behind the men, in keeping with Israelite law, and gleans the remaining sheafs left behind. Her humility and diligence attract the attention and admiration of Boaz, in whose fields she is allowed to glean.

Over time, the relationship between Ruth and Boaz strengthens until, one night, at the counsel of Naomi, Ruth approaches Boaz with a request for marriage because he is her near kinsman. Boaz signifies his agreement by extending his garment over Ruth symbolizing his willingness to protect and provide for her. They wed, and Ruth eventually becomes the great-grandmother of David, Israel's finest king. Although she was a Moabitess, forbidden by law to enter the holy temple, God had compassion on her and redeemed her. He honored her for her humility and willingness to serve others. In due season, He removed the shame of her widowhood and restored her to an honorable marriage. Furthermore, He released her to minister before the townspeople and participate in bringing forth ("birthing") the will of God (Ru 4:13–15).

Similarly, our woman at the well was a Samaritan. She had been "widowed" five times either through divorce or death. She was an outcast and a foreigner. However, somewhere in the midst of all her life's disappointments, she chose to trust the Lord and place her hope in his Messiah. As a result, she received the privilege of personal ministry. Jesus went out of his way to meet and restore her. Who knows what happened after that first encounter? I often wonder if Jesus returned to Sychar during his many trips back and forth from Galilee to Jerusalem. I wonder if the Samaritan woman came to the Cross or went on to become a home leader in the early Church.

Perhaps she was one of the many women whom Paul mentions in his epistles to early congregations. Perhaps she even became one of the early church martyrs—we do not know.

Whatever path she followed, the woman at the well, like Ruth, offers hope that God will receive anyone. The only requirement for his restoration is a yielded heart. He is the Potter; we are merely the clay (Is 64:8). He desires to pour out his Spirit on both men and women for prophecy and service in the Body of Christ (Jl 2:28).

Revelation 22:1–2 says, "Then the angel showed me the river of the water of life, clear as crystal, flowing from the throne of God and of the Lamb … On each side of the river stood the tree of life, bearing twelve crops of fruit, yielding its fruit every month. And the leaves of the tree are for the healing of the nations." Verse 17 adds, "The Spirit and the Bride say 'Come!' And let him who hears say 'Come!' Whoever is thirsty, let him come; and whoever wishes, let him take the free gift of the water of life."

This is our heritage. We host the springs through which God dispenses the living water of Jesus Christ to the world. Isaiah 61:3 calls us "oaks of righteousness," plantings of the Lord who never cease to bear fruit. We are the living pools of Bethesda, which, when stirred by the Spirit of God, bring healing to all who enter in (Jn 5:2–4). Our final destiny, our abiding purpose, involves becoming co-heirs with Christ of an immense, spiritual estate (Rom 8:17). We are called to be a nation of kings and priests, ministering and interceding daily before the Lord (Rv 5:10). In essence, we are restored in order to restore others. God desires to enable us to have our own "women at the well" encounters (1 Cor 5:17–18) and thereby participate with him in bringing forth the harvest—one life at a time.

Scripture Study

Read John 4:28-42.

1. What two analogies or parables does Jesus share with the disciples upon their return?

2. What key ideas is He trying to communicate through these analogies?

3. How do they fit into the story of the Samaritan woman?

4. Let's look more closely at these analogies individually. The first one deals with food. Specifically, what is the food to which Jesus refers? Why does this confuse the disciples?

5. How is this interplay between Jesus and the disciples similar to the verbal volleying that He experienced from the Samaritan woman earlier in this chapter (v. 11-15)?

The second analogy concerns the harvest. **Read John 4:35–38.**

6. What are the "fields" Christ is referring to?

Read John 6. There are several events taking place in this chapter.

1. What happens in verses 1–15?

2. Why does Jesus depart from the people?

3. What was the people's underlying motive for making him king?

4. What happens in verses 24–69?

5. Why do the people become offended at Jesus's words?

6. What does He mean by saying we must "eat his flesh and drink his blood"? How does this relate to Christ's teaching in John 15:1–8?

7. The word "abide" comes from the Greek word *meno* which means "to stay in a given place, state, relation, or expectancy." Practically speaking, how does one "abide" in Christ?

Read Matthew 20:1–16.
1. Who does the owner represent?

2. Who are the workers? What is significant about the number of hours each worker works?

3. If you interpreted this parable prophetically, with each group of workers representing different nations, where do you think America comes in?

4. What does Luke 9:51–62 suggest about the "cost" of our participation in the harvest?

Finally, turn to the book of Ruth. If you are not familiar with this book, I suggest you read it in its entirety. Otherwise, just glance over it to refresh your memory and answer the following questions:

1. Who are the main characters in this story?

2. What is the primary setting for the book?

3. What does Ruth's "gleaning" of the harvest fields represent?

4. What are the results of her humble service first to Naomi and then to Boaz? What sort of inheritance does she receive?

5. What parallels and symbols does this book share with the story of the Samaritan woman in John 4?

6. What do both accounts teach us about God's heart for restoration?

Reflection

In all honesty, what is your primary "food source"? Do you typically place more emphasis upon the natural or spiritual aspects of daily life? In what ways are you feeding your spirit daily? Are you abiding?

What fields are ripe in your life for harvest right now? Have you allowed the Lord of the harvest (Mt 9:36–38) to send you out? What, if anything, is holding you back?

What Scripture or teaching, from this entire study, has affected you most? How have you learned to relate to God more intimately? Where do you still wish to grow? Summarize in your journal what you have learned about your spiritual heritage as a woman of God.

Look back to your first journal entry. What was the one way you desired to grow through this study? How has the Lord answered that request?

Bibliography

American Heritage Dictionary. 2nd College Edition. Boston: Houghton Mifflin Company, 1985.

Bickle, Mike. *Passion for Jesus.* Lake Mary, Fla: Creation House, 1994.

Chapman, Gary. *The Five Love Languages.* Chicago: Moody Press, 1997.

Frangipane, Francis. *The Three Battlegrounds.* Cedar Rapids, Iowa: Arrow Publications, 1989.

Joyner, Rick. *The Final Quest.* New Kensington, Penn: Whitaker House, 1996.

Lambert, D.W., M.A. *Oswald Chambers: An Unbribed Soul.* Fort Washington, Penn: Christian Literature Crusade, 1989.

Savard, Liberty S. *Shattering Your Strongholds.* North Brunswick, NJ: Bridge-Logos Publishers, 1997.

Senter, Ruth. *Have We Really Come A Long Way? Regaining What Feminism Has Stolen From Christian Women.* Minneapolis, Minn: Bethany House Publishers, 1997.

Smith, Chuck. *Living Water: The Power of the Holy Spirit in Your Life.* Eugene, Ore: Harvest House Publishers, 1996.

About the Author

Julie R. Wilson has been writing and leading Bible studies for more than fifteen years. She joined FaithWalk Publishing in the fall of 2002. With the publication of *Restoring Your Spiritual Heritage*, Julie has completed six book-length studies. The other five are:

Homecoming: A Prophetic Study of Ruth (FaithWalk, 2002)
Companions of Hope: A Study of Biblical Hope (FaithWalk, 2003)
Born for Redemption: Overcoming Self-Condemnation
   (FaithWalk, 2005)
A Mother's Confession, A Father's Reply
A Woman Fully Clothed: Recovering Intimacy as the Bride
   of Christ

Julie served in leadership with the women's ministry of a large interdenominational church for five years, where she coordinated weekly Bible studies for approximately 250 women and conducted leadership training. She also served for three years as the coordinator of online Bible studies and devotionals for *SpiritLed Woman* magazine, a monthly publication of Strang Communications, reaching more than 350,000 believers.

A two-time Texas Tech grad (BA in comparative literature and MA in technical writing), Julie lives in Lubbock, Texas, with her husband, Keith, their children, Alexia and Samuel, their horses, and the family dog, Gimli. She enjoys teaching, preaching, and leading retreats.

For more information or a complete list of audio and print resources, please contact www.wellhouseministries.com.